Date Due

DUE DATE 12/19/05

PRINTED IN U.S.A.

A Short History of Literary Criticism

A SHORT HISTORY OF

Literary Criticism

By VERNON HALL, JR.

NEW YORK UNIVERSITY PRESS

Second Impression

© 1963 BY NEW YORK UNIVERSITY

LIBRARY OF CONGRESS CARD NUMBER: 63:17156

MANUFACTURED IN THE UNITED STATES OF AMERICA

For Anne-Marie and Walter

NOTE OF APPRECIATION

My students past and present in my course in the history of literary criticism at Dartmouth have managed to give me a good idea of what needs to be explained in the major critical texts of our tradition. My friends Oscar Cargill, Irving Ribner, Harry Schultz, T. S. K. Scott-Craig, and David Bradley have been kind enough to make helpful suggestions for the improvement of this book as to both form and content.

A KNOWLEDGE of the beliefs men have held, and still hold, about imaginative literature satisfies the natural curiosity that all thoughtful people have about the history of those ideas that have shaped their civilization. More importantly, however, such knowledge enables the reader to approach good literature with a deeper appreciation than he would otherwise have.

Whether certain critical principles enunciated in the past are valid for all time or not, the fact that they were believed to be true shaped both the form and determined the content of innumerable literary masterpieces. Thus an understanding of what a writer achieved often depends on an acquaintance with the critical doctrines he and his contemporaries assumed to be the foundation of art.

Yet, so many literary critics have practiced their trade that a complete history of literary criticism would either have to be impossibly long or would have to squeeze in so many names and dates as to be practically unreadable. This modest work, then, contents itself with offering a chart of the shifting currents of literary opinion. For clarity and brevity, the discussion of the individual critic is limited to one or two of his most important essays. Since, ideally, this commentary should be read in conjunction with the actual works of the critics themselves, an attempt has been made to limit, where possible, the observations to those essays most easily found in the standard anthologies.

Selective as such a little book as this must be, it will, the author hopes, serve as a useful and pleasant introduction to what Milton called the "sublime art."

CONTENTS

SINCE ALL QUOTATIONS are from the relatively short essays named in each chapter, and since my commentary usually follows the order of the author's thought, footnotes were considered unnecessary.

I have quoted from the following translations:

Plato: Benjamin Jowett (*Dialogues*, Oxford, 1892).

Aristotle: S. H. Butcher (Aristotle's *Theory of Poetry and Fine Art*, London, 1895).

Horace: Francis Howes (A. S. Cook, *The Art of Poetry*, Boston, 1892).

Longinus: W. Rhys Roberts (*On the Sublime*, Cambridge, 1907).

Dante: A. G. F. Howell and P. H. Wicksteed (*A Translation of the Latin Works of Dante*, London, 1904).

Boccaccio: A. H. Gilbert (*Literary Criticism: Plato to Dryden*, Detroit, 1962).

Boileau: Sir William Soames (A. S. Cook, *The Art of Poetry*, Boston, 1892).

Hugo: G. B. Ives (*Works of Victor Hugo*, New York, 1909).

Goethe: John Oxenford (*Goethe's Conversations with Eckermann*, London, 1901).

Sainte-Beuve: A. J. Butler (*Selected Essays of Sainte-Beuve*, London, n.d.).

Taine: H. van Laun (*History of English Literature*, Edinburg, 1873).

Zola: Belle M. Sherman (*The Experimental Novel and Other Essays*, New York, 1893).

France: Bernard Miall (*Life and Letters*, 4th Series, New York, 1924).

Brunetière: Philip M. Hayden (*Law of the Drama*, New York, 1914).

Tolstoy: Alymer Maude (*What Is Art? and Essays on Art*, London, 1938).

Bergson: C. Brereton and F. Rothwell (*Laughter: an Essay on the Meaning of the Comic*, London, 1911).

Croce: R. G. Collingwood ("Aesthetics," *Encyclopaedia Britannica*, 14th ed., New York, 1929), and A. H. Gilbert (G. W. Allen and H. H. Clark, *Literary Criticism: Pope to Croce*, Detroit, 1962).

A Short History of Literary Criticism

1 · Plato (427–347 B.C.)

THE GREEKS were great talkers and they must, among other things, have talked about poetry. Yet their words were carried away by the winds of the Mediterranean. Before Plato, except for a line or two in the poets and a few fragments from philosophical treatises, there was no real literary criticism in the sense of a theory of literature. Even the brilliant literary evaluations that Aristophanes makes in his comedies are practical rather than theoretical. So if we want to begin with general ideas on literature, we must begin with Plato. One could wish to begin elsewhere, for Plato, the most poetic of philosophers, was an enemy of poetry. This is a fact so shocking that many have refused to believe it. Like too naïve lovers they have refused the evidence of their own eyes. Honey-mouthed Plato could not be unfaithful.

Yet the case is clear. As Tolstoy is going to find later, Plato found that he had to betray his own art because he had discovered something he believed to be greater. Saint Augustine will read him and use him to strengthen the antagonism of the early Christian Church to literature. The political totalitarians of the twentieth century, both communist and fascist, are going to borrow his approach. Everyone who believes he has found the TRUTH will fall into Plato's position toward art. If one's sole concern is building the Platonic Republic, the Soviet State, or the City of God, literature must be done away with or put in chains. What is a poem compared with man's immortal soul or the classless society?

From every point of view he took, pedagogical, metaphysical,

1

ethical, or political, Plato arrived at the same sobering conclusion—poetry is dangerous. The puritan streak in him even, we
suspect, found melancholy satisfaction in giving up what he
loved. For Plato loved poetry, or he would not have feared it so.
Thomas Mann's short stories and novels, where art is presented
time and time again as the seducer, the disintegrator of our
middle-class morality, are, among other things, deep-seeing com-
mentaries on Plato and the poets.

Heavy with civilization as we are, we picture Plato as living
in the fresh dawn of our culture. To him, of course, it seemed
like the sunset. The great things had already been done. Athens
was rushing to destruction. A Mediterranean people, art-loving
and soft, were being led like sheep by unscrupulous demagogues.
For religion they had the gods and goddesses as represented in
Homer: fornicators, liars, and quarrelers. What the Athenian
needed desperately was the discipline and reason that could be
supplied by philosophers like Plato.

The poets, living and dead, were Plato's enemies. Everyone
accepted the fact that they were teachers. The poets, as all
agreed, were inspired. This, Plato felt, was enough to damn
them, for is not truth arrived at by reason? In the *Ion* he gave
the popular theory of poetry.

For the poet is a light and winged and holy thing, and there is no
invention in him until he has been inspired and is out of his senses,
and then the mind is no longer in him: when he has not attained
to this state, he is powerless and is unable to utter his oracles. Many
are the noble words in which poets speak of actions like your own
words about Homer; but they do not speak of them by any rules of
art: only when they make that to which the Muse impels them are
their inventions inspired; and then one of them will make dithy-
rambs, another hymns of praise, another choral strains, another
epic or iambic verses—and he who is good at one is not good at
any other kind of verse; for not by art does the poet sing, but by
power divine.

This apparently noble conception of poetry he then turned
against the poets. The charioteer knows more about chariot-
racing than Homer. Every artisan knows more about his own
craft than the poet who speaks of his craft. Thus, as a teacher
the poet is inferior to the artisan. Since, then, the poet speaks,
not from knowledge but from inspiration (or madness—for

Plato it is much the same thing), he cannot be trusted as a teacher.

The poet fared no better when examined in the light of Plato's metaphysics. According to Plato, reality existed in the world of Ideas, not in the world of material things. There was, for instance, the Idea of the bed, the real and unchanging bed. The individual bed that the cabinetmaker constructed was an imitation, by definition imperfect, of the ideal bed. When the poet described a bed he was imitating an imitation and was thus two degrees removed from truth or reality. The poet's art was "an inferior who marries an inferior and has inferior offspring."

For morality and ethics, the citizen had better go almost anywhere rather than to the poets. In Homer, God is represented as doing things which are morally wrong. Zeus arbitrarily assigns happiness to some, unhappiness to others. Athene and Zeus are represented as the violators of oaths and treaties, other gods as the causers of evil and strife among men. Since God is good, evil must have another cause. Thus, not only does Homer lie about the gods, but his poetry can lead the citizen into the paths of wickedness. The poet should be prevented by law from saying that God causes evil.

And if a poet writes of the sufferings of Niobe—the subject of the tragedy in which these iambic verses occur—or of the house of Pelops, or of the Trojan war or any similar theme, either we must not permit him to say that these are the works of God, or if they are of God, he must devise some explanation of them such as we are seeking; he must say that God did what was just and right, and they were the better for being punished; but that those who are punished are miserable, and that God is the author of their misery— the poet is not to be permitted to say; though he may say that the wicked are miserable because they require to be punished, and are benefitted by receiving punishment from God; but that God being good is the author of evil to any one is to be strenuously denied, and not to be said or sung or heard in verse or prose by any one whether old or young in any well-ordered commonwealth. Such a fiction is suicidal, ruinous, impious. (*Republic*)

Ethics and politics cannot, for Plato, be disentangled. In attempting to set up an education for the future rulers or guardians of his ideal Republic, he finds that the poets do not teach good citizenship. Not only do they lie about the gods, but they represent men as doing unworthy things. They show heroes sulking in their tents, magistrates taking bribes, and many other things which soldiers and rulers should not consider even possible. Particularly evil is their representation of Hades as a shadowy, unpleasant place. Young men should be taught to die bravely for their country, with the promise of reward in the afterlife. The Hades of the poets is a deterrent to heroism and makes young men cowards, desirous of life, and fearful of death. Members of the ruling class, the guardians, should dedicate themselves wholly to the maintenance of freedom in the state and should not imitate anything vile.

Yet, what examples would the poets give them? Women, bad men, even low characters such as "smiths or other artificers or oarsmen, or boat-swains, or the like." Indeed, all things that seem pleasant to the ignorant multitude. Nor must we forget that poetry feeds and waters the passions that ought to be dried up. "She lets them rule, although they ought to be controlled, if mankind are ever to increase in happiness and virtue."

When the poet who can imitate anything comes to the city, "we will fall down and worship him as a sweet and holy and wonderful being; but we must also inform him that in our State such as he are not permitted to exist; the law will not allow them. And so when we have anointed him with myrrh, and set a garland of wool upon his head, we shall send him away to another city."

Thus the poet is exiled from Plato's Republic.

Is there then to be no song, no poetry? Some, but only that written under the control of the rulers. Music which makes for good military discipline; hymns to the gods and praises for good men. But even this official poetry cannot be written by anyone. Only the politically reliable, to use a modern term, may write. And even they will be limited to "official" poetry. So the victors in the games that strengthen the state may be praised, but not by every poet.

And let poets celebrate the victors,—not however every poet, but only one who in the first place is not less than fifty years of age; nor should he be one who, although he may have musical and poetical gifts, has never in his life done any noble or illustrious action; but those who are themselves good and also honourable in the state, creators of noble actions—let their poems be sung, even though they be not very musical. And let the judgment of them rest with the instructor of youth (i.e., the director of education) and the other guardians of the laws, who shall give them this privilege, and they alone shall be free to sing; but the rest of the world shall not have this liberty. Nor shall any one dare to sing a song which has not been approved by the judgment of the guardians of the laws, not even if his strain be sweeter than the songs of Thamyras and Orpheus; but only such poems as have been judged sacred and dedicated to the gods, and such as are the works of good men, in which praise or blame has been awarded and which have been deemed to fulfill their design fairly. (*Laws*)

BIBLIOGRAPHY

Atkins, John W. H. *Literary Criticism in Antiquity: A Sketch of its Development.* 2 vols. Cambridge, 1934.

Collingwood, R. G. *The Principles of Art.* Oxford, 1938.

Grube, G. M. A. *Plato's Thought.* London, 1935.

Plato. *Dialogues*; tr. by Lane Cooper. New York, 1938.

———. *Dialogues*; tr. by Benjamin Jowett. Oxford, 1892.

———. *Dialogues* (Loeb Classics Series). Cambridge, 1917–1935.

———. *Laws*; tr. by A. E. Taylor. London, 1934.

———. *Œuvres complètes, publiées sous le patronage de l'Association Guillaume Budé.* Paris, 1920.

Shorey, Paul. *What Plato Said.* Chicago, 1933.

Taylor, A. E. *Plato.* London, 1929.

2 · Aristotle (384–322 B.C.)

REGARDLESS of what one may think of Plato's critical theories, it must be admitted that he formulated many of the major problems of literary criticism. And it is to his credit, too, that it was his pupil, Aristotle, who gave, in the opinion of most future critics, the best answers to the questions Plato had raised. By the time Aristotle turned his mind to the analysis of literature, the future of Athens, with which Plato was so concerned, had already been decided. Henceforth, she was to be a second-rate power. Political and social problems could no longer have the urgency that they had had in Plato's time. This enabled Aristotle to consider more calmly the questions that had agitated his teacher.

Though what Plato had said was always in the back of his mind, Aristotle—and this was his great genius—found what he was looking for, not by putting his own metaphysical generalizations against those of his master, but by examining literature itself in the same way that he examined biological specimens when he wrote his work on animals. It was not his fault that his descriptions and perceptions later hardened into rules. Indeed, his whole method is a rebuke of those who set up absolute standards and attempt to make works of art fit them.

The very beginning of his *Poetics* gives us the promise of an examination of literature free from Plato's preconceptions. Aristotle sees that epic poetry, tragedy, comedy, dithyrambic poetry, and music are alike in that they all *imitate*. They differ in the medium, objects, and manner of imitation. All except music imitate with language in metrical form, but, he hastens to point

6

out, Empedocles cannot be given the name of poet merely because he wrote his natural philosophy in meter. The poet imitates men, men who are in action, and who are better or worse than we are. "The same distinction marks off Tragedy from Comedy; for Comedy aims at representing men as worse, Tragedy as better, than in actual life."

Poetry has two reasons for being. First, man is an imitative animal and takes pleasure in imitation. "We have evidence of this in the facts of experience. Objects which in themselves we view with pain, we delight to contemplate when reproduced with minute fidelity; such as the forms of the most ignoble animals and of dead bodies. The cause of this again is, that to learn gives the liveliest pleasure, not only to philosophers but to men in general; whose capacity, however, of learning is more limited." Equally natural and pleasant to man is the second reason for poetry: harmony and rhythm.

For Plato the pleasure that comes from imitation and rhythm could be dangerous and undermine the civic virtues. Aristotle does not discuss this contention for the moment. At this point in his argument he only wants to show that it is natural to imitate and to get pleasure from imitation.

Aristotle follows his master in believing that the higher the subject matter the higher the type of poem. "The graver spirits imitated noble actions, and the actions of good men. The more trivial sort imitated the actions of meaner persons, at first composing satires, as the former did hymns to the gods and the praises of famous men." From a modern point of view this seems to contradict the view he has just expressed that pleasure comes from the quality of imitation regardless of the object imitated. It is perhaps a hangover from the austere scorn of Plato. This may account for the fact that Aristotle dismisses comedy in a word or two as "an imitation of characters of a lower type—not, however, in the full sense of the word bad, the ludicrous being merely a subdivision of the ugly."

Aristotle's major interest is in tragedy, which he defines as "an imitation of an action that is serious, complete, and of a certain magnitude; in language embellished with each kind of artistic ornament, the several kinds being found in separate parts of the play; in the form of action, not of narrative; through pity and fear effecting the proper purgation [catharsis] of these emotions." This famous definition has exercised the minds of many men, some of whom are frank enough to admit that the feeling they have at the end of a great tragedy is not akin to the feeling of having been purged of these emotions. No doubt Aristotle felt that he had to answer Plato's charge that drama aroused emotion in men's hearts and was therefore capable of making them more emotional and less rational. He hit upon the idea of claiming that tragedy purges us of emotions. He would have been on better ground if he had claimed—in accord with his emphasis on form—that the true tragedy gives *form* to our emotions and thus *controls* them, making of them something far removed from the dangerous, uncontrolled emotions Plato feared.

This perhaps is implied. At any rate, the idea of form is Aristotle's greatest contribution to literary criticism. Unlike Plato, who identified poetry with its subject matter, he sees that the difference between a tragedy and life is that a tragedy has a beginning, a middle, and an end, and that each part ideally has a relation to every other part. This might be called logical form. But there is an ethical form, too. The tragic hero is "a man who is not eminently good and just, yet whose misfortune is brought about not by vice or depravity, but by some error or frailty. He must be one who is highly renowned and prosperous,—a personage like Oedipus, Thyestes, or other illustrious men of such families." Thus the tragic hero has a flaw, even if it is not his fault, and when he falls into bad fortune our sense of justice is not shocked. This dovetails with the emotional form we mentioned when speaking of the effect of tragedy. That the hero must be of a great family was believed not only by Aristotle but by most critics and playwrights down to our own day.

This emphasis on form enables him to answer Plato's slander that the poet is mad. The art of poetry is the art of the gifted man rather than the madman. For the poet must enter into the nature of his characters' sufferings and feel their distress and anger before he can imitate them. No man who is beside himself with madness can do so.

Aristotle is careful to answer all of Plato's important attacks. As to the charge that the poet tells lies and errs when, for instance, he describes a chariot race less correctly than a charioteer, Aristotle contends that the standard of what is correct is not the same in the art of poetry as it is in the art of life or any other art. The only error that is important occurs when the poet fails because he lacks imitative ability. But if he makes a mistake about medicine or something in any other profession, it is not a poetic error. In other words, Aristotle answers the Socrates of *Ion* in the way Ion himself should have answered. The purpose or end of poetry is not the same as the purpose of the man who teaches chariot-racing.

Aristotle is also careful to answer Plato's metaphysical objection that the poet in imitating the object (which is merely an imitation of the ideal) is two removes from the truth. He points out that poetry is more universal than things as they are. "It is not the function of the poet to relate what has happened, but what may happen—what is possible according to the law of probability or necessity." Thus he makes his famous distinction between history and poetry: The historian writes of what has already happened; the poet writes of what could happen. "Poetry, therefore, is a more philosophical and a higher thing than history: for poetry tends to express the universal, history the particular." Thus it is that in poetry a probable impossibility is more acceptable than an incredible possibility. This implies that the poet, rather than merely imitating things in nature, as Plato said he did, actually attains nearer to the Ideal. For, Aristotle insists, poets present things, not as they are, but as they should be. This emphasis on the universal, though primarily intended as an answer to Plato, is implicit in Aristotle's whole view of literature.

Since poetry deals with the universal, the poet's characters as well as the poet's plots should be universal. This conception molded all classical tragedy, whether of Aristotle's time or that of Louis XIV. When he speaks of character, he says that goodness is relative to each class of people. "Even a woman may be good, and also a slave; though the woman may be said to be an inferior being, and the slave quite worthless." Obviously, the poet who follows these suggestions is going to make his kings good in the way men and kings are good, not in the way women and slaves are. This emphasis distinguishes classical art from romantic and realistic art. The king who does not act like a king finds his place in both romantic and realistic writings either because their authors want to be striking and original or because they want to give a slice of life, as we shall see in later chapters.

Obviously, Aristotle writes not of all drama but of the Greek drama he knew. The literature he writes about is already in the past and limited to one people and to one language. He, like most of the ancients, has little sense of history. Yet we, neither Platonists nor Aristotelians, but moderns, can use our own historical sense to prevent ourselves from blaming him for not doing things no man of his age could have done. His remarkable achievement remains. He tells us more true things about the literature of all ages, if not all literature, than any critic who has ever lived.

The more one reads the *Poetics*, the more one is impressed that Aristotle's fundamental reason for writing was to answer Plato. This he did superlatively. We have to thank Plato, the enemy of poetry, for inspiring its most brilliant defense.

BIBLIOGRAPHY

Albeggiani, Ferdinando. *La Poetica, traduzione, introduzione, commento*. Florence, 1934.

Aristotle. *The Basic Works*; ed. by Richard McKeon. New York, 1941.

Baldwin, Charles S. *Ancient Rhetoric and Poetic*. New York, 1924.

Butcher, S. H. *Aristotle's Theory of Poetry and Fine Art*. London, 1923.

Bywater, Ingram. *Aristotle on the Art of Poetry*. Oxford, 1909.

Cooper, Lane. *The Poetics of Aristotle*. Boston, 1923.

Cooper, Lane, and Alfred Gudeman. *A Bibliography of the Poetics of Aristotle*. New Haven, 1928.

Fyfe, W. H. *Aristotle, The Poetics*. London, 1927.

Herrick, M. T. *The Poetics of Aristotle in England*. New Haven, 1930.

Margoliouth, D. S. *The Poetics of Aristotle*. London, 1911.
Potts, L. J. *Aristotle on the Art of Fiction*. Cambridge, 1953.
Roberts, W. R. *Greek Rhetoric and Literary Theory*. New York, 1928.
Ross, W. D. *Aristotle*. London, 1930.
Rostagni, Augusto. *La Poetica di Aristotele*. Torino, 1934.

3 · Horace (65–8 B.C.)

ATHENS FADED, the empire of Alexander passed away, Rome now ruled the world. The greatest of Roman critics, Horace, lived at a time when all seemed settled once and for all. He was a friend of Augustus, whose reign promised universal and enduring peace. Nothing in his situation at Rome or in his own temperament could fan any spark of rebellion in him. His letter to the Pisos, called the *Art of Poetry*, thus becomes the handbook for all those who live in, or earnestly desire, a stable, aristocratic society. Throughout the Renaissance and neoclassical period he is the most influential of critics. Aristotle may be put on a pedestal, but it is Horace who is most often quoted and paraphrased.

His *Art of Poetry* is what one might expect from one whose own poetry was preeminently the poetry of good sense. He prefers, like all conservatives, the things of the past that have stood the test of time: old wine and Greek literature. He advises those who would be poets to thumb the Greek masterpieces day and night. He is against extremes. Purple patches, however eloquent, are to be omitted from the simple and consistent poetry that he writes and wants others to write. Too much originality is dangerous. It may make the poet bring impossible figures into his poem—"like a sick man's dreams." Though Horace recognizes that the poet must be an artist and that mere avoidance of faults is not enough, he nevertheless emphasizes the faults to be avoided. The poet must walk the middle path between terseness and obscurity, grandeur and bombast. The choice of the right theme will help the poet in finding the proper words and a lucid arrangement. His vocabulary should be moderate. He may coin words but sparingly and then only if he draws from a Greek source.

For Plato and Aristotle, imitation meant the imitation of nature. In Horace it begins to mean the imitation of other writers. We are told to look not so much at what is around us as at the poets who wrote in the past. Thus the matter and manner for epics has been set by Homer for all time.

Most important in any stable society is etiquette or decorum. Above all things, the poet must avoid being ridiculous. And nothing, unless it is intentional, is more ridiculous than allowing a speaker of one class to speak in the language of another:

> But if the actor play not to the life,
> If with his words his fortunes seem at strife,
> His knights and commons, horse and foot, shall scoff,
> And tittering thousands hoot the blunderer off.
> Each speaker let his speech characterize:
> For sure a broad and glaring difference lies,
> Whether a god or hero mount the stage;
> The brisk young spark or man mature in age;
> The dame of rank or nurse of prattling vein;
> The wandering seaman or the peaceful swain;
> One that Assyria or that Colchis fed;
> He that at Argos or at Thebes was bred.

Either stick to tradition, Horace advises, or see that your inventions be consistent. And it is safer to stick to tradition. Your credit will be greater if you treat hackneyed themes in a new way, instead of attempting to invent. First, there is a satisfaction in the old themes; second, the real charm of literature comes from your ability to see old things in a new way. And above all aim your sights low. Let no one be able to say the mountain labored and brought forth a mouse.

What in Aristotle were observations on poetic practices become rules in Horace. Since Homer began his epic in the middle of the action, Horace demands that the epic poet should begin *in medias res*.

Since Aristotle dealt largely with tragedy, so does Horace, though he was not a dramatic poet. He advocates the use of universal characters so that the spectator can know immediately what to expect. Children are quick to anger and quick to cool;

the young boy likes horses and dogs and the open fields. The old man is lazy, wants to live a long time, praises the past as it was "when he was a boy," and criticizes everything new. That all boys and young men are not alike did not concern Horace. The stereotyped boys and ancients of the Greek and Roman stage were much the same. This enables the dramatist to make plots without characters, something at least more workable, as Aristotle knew, than characters without plot.

Whereas Aristotle seemed to allow violence on the stage, Horace has become too polished to accept it. Any violence must be reported by a messenger and not shoved under the noses of the audience. For Aristotle a play should be long enough to do what it set out to do; for Horace it should consist of five acts. This rule of Horace solved a difficulty neatly, if dogmatically. Henceforth plays, all plays, must have five acts. Etiquette becomes more important than drama; Horace specifically forbids the poet the license that Shakespeare was to make use of in *Henry IV*, that of allowing a prince's discourse to sink to the level of tavern talk.

More important than inspiration is labor. Roman poets could equal the fame of Roman generals if they did not scorn "the long labor of the file." The poem that has not been polished so that it is smooth to the fingernail is unworthy of Rome. Obviously, Horace had no sympathy with the bohemian or beatnik poet.

> There are in whom a wonderous whim prevails
> Neither to trim their beard nor pare their nails;
> Where crowded baths invite, they come not nigh,
> But to lone caves and silent deserts fly.
> For oh! he shines a bard confessed, be sure,
> Whose poll (which three Anticyras could not cure)
> To barber Licinus was ne'er consigned.

The writer of gentlemanly poetry must be a gentleman.

"The secret of all good writing," says Horace, "is sound judgment." The Latin word here is *sapere*, which includes both wisdom and learning, and however Horace meant it, later generations believed he meant that the poet should be learned.

The charm of poetry, he continues, does not necessarily exist for its own sake alone. The poet should try to blend together the delightful and the useful. Teaching is his business, but teaching with pleasure. Here Horace formulates the sugar-coated-pill theory of poetry, and the followers of Horace will echo the theory again and again.

So writes the aristocratic poet of ancient Rome. Hard work rather than genius, moderation rather than imagination. His prescriptions have virtue, and, if they leave out much that the Romantics are going to consider the very essence of poetry, they will be held as precious by the men of the Renaissance and the neoclassical age.

BIBLIOGRAPHY

Blakeney, E. H. *Horace on the Art of Poetry*. London, 1928.
Cook, A. S. *The Art of Poetry*. New York, 1926.
D'Alton, J. F. *Horace and His Age*. London, 1917.
———. *Roman Literary Theory and Criticism*. London and New York, 1931.
Fairclough, H. R. *Horace, Satires, Epistles, and Ars Poetica* (Loeb Classics). New York, 1926.
Fiske, G. C. *Lucilius and Horace, a Study*. Madison, Wisc., 1920.
Rostagni, Augusto. *Arte poetica di Orazio*. Torino, 1930.
Showerman, Grant. *Horace and His Influence*. Boston, 1922.
Wilkinson, L. P. *Horace and His Lyric Poetry*. Cambridge, 1945.

4 · Longinus (First or Third Century A.D.)

WHO LONGINUS WAS, or what he wrote, are matters that have never been settled. Perhaps they are unimportant. What is important is that he was one of the greatest critics who ever lived. It was long thought that he was the secretary of Zenobia, third-century Queen of Palmyra, who stood for a time against the might of Rome. More recent scholarship, without identifying him, has tended to place him earlier, in the last part of the first century A.D. Yet, he is so far removed from Horace in spirit that one would like to put him as far away as possible in date too. Add to this the fact that he mentions Hebrew literature and is filled with something very like the neo-Platonism of Plotinus and one cannot but help feel, though no more than feel, that he belongs more to the third century than to the first.

Even the title of his work has never been translated to the satisfaction of everyone. The traditional translation, *On the Sublime,* has been objected to as having a false connotation in English, and such titles as "the height of eloquence" and "on literary excellence" have been suggested. Wordsworth wrote, "Longinus treats of animated, impassioned, energetic, or, if you will, elevated writing." Yet, if we use "sublime" in the widest sense, we are perhaps justified in keeping the traditional title. The important thing is not the title but the treatise itself.

When we come to Longinus we have a man who can properly be considered as not only the first Romantic critic, but also the first comparative critic. Although it was not unknown in Rome to compare Greek and Latin literature, these two were always

16

so closely intertwined that we can hardly dignify such a comparison with the name of comparative. It is when Longinus quotes from Genesis and thus brings into play a literature in an entirely different tradition that we have the first real critic of general literature. From his name we know he was Greek. From his dates, whether we accept the first or third century, we know that he was a Greek at a time when Greece had lost all political power and had no hope of power in the future. As a result, Longinus looks at literature, most of which is far in the past, in much the same way as we look at Homer, Tasso, and Milton. He is free from immediate political and ethical considerations.

His letter, addressed to his friend Postumius Terentianus, is the first treatise written from the point of view of the teacher, the reviewer of great literature, rather than from that of the philosopher, the analyzer, or the recipe-maker. The literature he is interested in is that which has given him pleasure. Like a man talking to a friend of similar taste, he quotes those passages which seem to him to be of the highest literary excellence and explains their excellence. Unlike Aristotle, he is not interested in the natural history of literature, or in the tragedy or the epic. He is interested in the phrase or passage which strikes fire from his mind. Form in the larger sense is no longer important. It is the individual short poems or the individual passage which he, in the manner of the more modern critics, explains.

He defines sublimity by showing that it consists of

a certain distinction and excellence in expression, and that it is from no other source than this that the greatest poets and writers have derived their eminence and gained an immortality of renown. The effect of elevated language upon an audience is not persuasion but transport. At every time and in every way imposing speech, with the spell it throws over us, prevails over that which aims at persuasion and gratification. Our persuasions we can usually control, but the influences of the sublime bring power and irresistible might to bear, and reign over every hearer. Similarly, we see skill in invention, and due order and arrangement of matter, emerging as the hard-won result not of one thing nor of two, but of the whole texture of the composition, whereas Sublimity flashing forth at the right moment scatters everything before it like a thunderbolt, and at once displays the power of the orator in all its plentitude.

Although admitting that curbs on genius are needed, so that the poet will not write bombast, he is interested mainly in the genius which transcends all rules.

Unfortunately, at this point there is a lacuna in the original manuscript. When it begins again, Longinus is speaking of faults to be avoided. He gives examples of the false sublime, bombast, puerility, ill-timed pathos, and frigidity. Here, once more, he measures these things not by rules but by the touchstone of his own taste. He is worried about the craze for novelty which sprang up in his age as it springs up during the decline of every literary period. But there is no easy way to avoid this pitfall. He points out that an accurate judgment in literature results only from long experience. Only those with this experience can distinguish between the true and the false. He then says:

For, as if instinctively, our soul is uplifted by the true sublime; it takes a proud flight, and is filled with joy and vaunting, as though it had itself produced what it has heard. When, therefore, a thing is heard repeatedly by a man of intelligence, who is well versed in literature, and its effect is not to dispose the soul to high thoughts, and it does not leave in the mind more food for reflexion than the words seem to convey, but falls, if examined carefully through and through, into disesteem; it cannot rank as true sublimity because it does not survive a first hearing. For that is really great which bears a repeated examination, and which it is difficult or rather impossible to withstand, and the memory of which is strong and hard to efface. In general, consider those examples of sublimity to be fine and genuine which please all and always. For when men of different pursuits, lives, ambitions, ages, languages, hold identical views on one and the same subject, then that verdict which results, so to speak, from a concert of discordant elements makes our faith in the object of admiration strong and unassailable.

This definition of true excellence has been quoted many times. Whether, indeed, it is possible for any literary passage to please all men in all ages has become more doubtful as we learn more about cultures with other traditions. To take an obvious example, we accept the excellence of classical Chinese music on the word of our Chinese friends. It does not please us. Nevertheless, within our own tradition, Longinus' definition contains at least a germ of the truth.

Longinus then gives five fountains of eloquence in an attempt to clarify his definition. They are:

1] A firm grasp of ideas
2] Vehement and inspired emotion
3] The proper construction of figures
4] Notable language
5] General effect of dignity and elevation

He seems to quarrel with Aristotle's theory of catharsis when he tells us that there are some feelings that are mean and devoid of sublimity, such as pity, worry, and fear. Indeed, his statement that true excellence exalts us seems opposed to Aristotle's famous definition of tragedy.

In the second part of his work, Longinus takes up each of the five sources of excellence. To have great ideas one must have greatness. "Sublimity is the echo of a great soul. . . . For it is not possible that men with mean and servile ideas and aims prevailing throughout their lives should produce anything that is admirable and worthy of immortality." As an example of the sublimity that comes from great ideas, he quotes, "the legislator of the Jews, no ordinary man," as writing, "*God said,—*what? *Let there be light, and there was light; let there be land, and there was land.*" In this section, which is of extreme interest, he compares the *Odyssey* and the *Iliad*. He then quotes a great poem of Sappho and preserves it for posterity.

It is impossible to describe all the many excellencies of this treatise. His important lesson is that we can be sure of the greatness of a given passage when intellect, senses, and will respond together. Longinus does not, of course, escape certain faults of his age. He spends much time on faults of diction which we would consider better spent on other things. But even in so doing, he gives us more examples of his taste. He believes that sublimity is recognizable because within each of us is a power which aspires toward the great and the noble.

Nature has appointed us men to be no base or ignoble animals; but when she ushers us into life and into the vast universe as into some great assembly, to be as it were spectators of the mighty whole and the keenest aspirants for honour, forthwith she implants in our souls the unconquerable love of whatever is elevated and more divine than we.

All of this is as unneoclassical, as un-Horatian as possible. As Longinus says, "Correctness escapes censure: greatness earns admiration as well."

He concludes his treatise by wondering, since in his own time there is little of excellence, whether Greek literature went out with democracy and whether freedom alone is able "to foster intellectual genius and to fill it with high hopes." We suspect that he felt that the answer might be yes, for his disclaimer, although true enough for his own time, does not hit at the heart of the matter. He writes:

It is easy, my good sir, and characteristic of human nature, to find fault with the age in which one lives. But consider whether it may not be true that it is not the world's peace that ruins great natures, but far rather this war illimitable which holds our desires in its grasp, aye, and further still those passions which occupy as with troops our present age and utterly harry and plunder it. For the love of money (a disease from which we all now suffer sorely) and the love of pleasure make us their thralls, or rather, as one may say, drown us body and soul in the depths, the love of riches being a malady which makes men petty, and the love of pleasure one which makes them most ignoble.

Then after a few more remarks, the manuscript breaks off. How much we have lost we will, perhaps, never know, but what we have contains a spirit of criticism that we should not want to be without.

BIBLIOGRAPHY

Henn, T. R. *Longinus and English Criticism*. Cambridge, 1934.
Longinus. *On Elevation of Style*; tr. by T. G. Tucker. London, 1935.
———. *On the Sublime*; tr. by W. H. Fyfe. New York, 1927.
Monk, S. H. *The Sublime: A Study of Critical Theories in Eighteenth-Century England*. New York, 1935.
Roberts, W. R. *Longinus on the Sublime*. Cambridge, 1935.

5·Dante (1265–1321)

THE MIDDLE AGES are no longer considered a period of Gothic darkness. Such a neoclassical prejudice was destroyed by the Romantic movement. Year by year our appreciation for the art and literature of the medieval creators has grown. Yet, for the historian of literary criticism, the period is still the Dark Ages. With the exception of Dante no critic can be found who is worth mentioning in so short a book as this.

Nor is this surprising. With philosophy primarily concerned with theological problems and with all other intellectual activity subordinated, at least in theory, to theology, it is obvious that the kind of literary criticism we found in Aristotle and Longinus could not be written. From the time of Saint Augustine on, the reading of the literary classics was looked upon by a large number of people as either a waste of time or as actually dangerous to one's immortal soul. When they were mentioned with approval it was usually as moral and religious allegories. Vergil would have been surprised to discover that his medieval readers thought that he had predicted the birth of Christ and that the *Aeneid* could be read as an allegory of the soul's search for salvation.

Dante's letter to Can Grande Della Scala, which was seemingly given to the great lord as an introduction to the *Paradiso*, shows us that even this most learned of poets knew little or nothing of classical criticism. As a result he was forced to employ the terms of scholastic philosophy instead of those worked out by Aristotle and Horace. His achievement shows that literary criticism is possible outside of the classical vocabulary. Strange as his criticism sounds, it is very much to the point.

Therefore if we desire to furnish some introduction to a part of any work, it behooves us to furnish some knowledge of the whole of which it is a part. Wherefore I, too, desiring to furnish something by way of introduction to the above-named portion of the *Comedy*, have thought that something concerning the whole work should be premised, that the approach to the part should be the easier and more complete. There are six things then which must be inquired into at the beginning of any work of instruction; to wit, the *subject, agent, form,* and *end,* the *title of the work,* and *branch of philosophy* it concerns. And there are three of these wherein this part which I purposed to design for you differs from the whole; to wit, *subject, form,* and *title;* whereas in the others it differs not, as is plain on inspection. And so, an inquiry concerning these three must be instituted specially with reference to the work as a whole; and when this has been done the way will be sufficiently clear to the introduction of the part. After that we shall examine the other three, not only with reference to the whole but also with reference to that special part which I am offering to you.

He then explains that his *Comedy* is "polysemous," that is, that it has many meanings.

The first is called literal, but the second allegorical or mystic. And this mode of treatment, for its better manifestation, may be considered in this verse: "When Israel came out of Egypt, and the house of Jacob from a people of strange speech, Judah became his sanctification, Israel his power." For if we inspect the letter alone the departure of the children of Israel from Egypt in the time of Moses is presented to us; if the allegory, our redemption wrought by Christ; if the moral sense, the conversion of the soul from the grief and misery of sin to the state of grace is presented to us; if the anagogical, the departure of the holy soul from the slavery of this corruption to the liberty of eternal glory is presented to us. And although these mystic senses have each their special denominations, they may all in general be called allegorical, since they differ from the literal and historical; for allegory is derived from *alleon,* in Greek, which means the same as the Latin *alienum* or *diversum.*

A careful study of his *Comedy* will show that not only the poem as a whole but each episode has these four levels of meaning.

Dante calls his work a comedy because it begins horribly (with Hell) and ends pleasingly (with Heaven). The classical distinction between tragedy and comedy has been thus simplified. Since it is a comedy, the mode of expression is the speech of the people. The purpose of the work is to "remove those living in this life from the state of misery and lead them to the state of felicity." Thus his *Comedy* fulfills the Horatian prescription to teach and delight as the Middle Ages understood it. The teaching is ethical or Christian; the delight comes from the adornment of words and from the fact that goodness in itself is delightful, as he points out in a critical passage in another work, his *Convivio*.

Dante accepted scholastic modes of thought and found nothing to object to in them. Working successfully with them, he had no desire to find different modes. But another question, that of language, existed which required of him a treatise which is like nothing written by his contemporaries. It is of the greatest interest and value.

Its title, which is given either as *De vulgari eloquentia* or as *De vulgari eloquio*, is translated as *On the Vulgar Tongue*. In it Dante comes to grips with a problem vital to his interests, the question of whether it is possible to have worthy literature in the mother tongue. Most educated men of his time wrote in Latin and felt that the vernacular was not suitable for their purposes. Could the vulgar tongue be made good enough to compete with Latin?

The problem was not an easy one. There was no Italian tongue. There were merely dialects, each of which differed from the other not only in pronunciation but in vocabulary. Dante realized that no one dialect would do. An illustrious vernacular had to be constructed. If it were, it would aid Dante's political dream. He believed in the possibility of uniting all Italians under the Holy Roman Emperor and was in exile from Florence because of his politics. The establishment of a common language for the whole peninsula would make political unity easier.

Since he is writing from a universal rather than a local point of view, Dante examines all of the vernaculars before choosing the one best fitted for his purpose. He accepts Hebrew as the best since it is the language of Adam, but he limits his search for the illustrious vernacular to the languages of Europe. Among the language groups he gives his preference to the Romance. This group is divided according to the word for "yes." The Provençals say "oc," (Dante calls them Spaniards—the part of Spain which produced the literature Dante knew used Provençal for literary purpose), the French "oïl," and the Italians "si." "Italian"—though he does not use this term—is best since the Italian "si" is nearest to the Latin adverb of affirmation "sic" and the best poets write in this vernacular.

Dante now carefully examines the various dialects of Italian. Many are quickly dismissed as being too rough, or too smooth, or too barbarous. Of those worthy of longer consideration, Sicilian ranks first. This is because of the patronage of Frederick the Emperor and his son Manfred. Yet the language of the Sicilian court poets is not, he makes clear, that of the common people. He says:

If we accept the Sicilian dialect, that, namely, spoken by the common people, from whose speech it appears our judgment should be drawn, we shall find that it is nowise worthy of preference. . . . If however, we decline to accept this dialect but choose in preference that spoken by the highest Sicilians . . . [we shall find] that it differs in nothing from that language which is the most worthy of praise, as we shall show further on.

After discussing and dismissing the other dialects, including his own native Florentine, Dante decides that no one dialect will do. The language he is searching for must be illustrious, cardinal, courtly, and curial. It belongs to all the towns of Italy but not exclusively to any one of them and is the standard against which all local dialects must be measured.

This illustrious vernacular is not the speech of the common people. It is the language of that Imperial court which Dante wants Italy to have.

Now the reason we call it Courtly is as follows: if we Italians had a Court it would be an Imperial one, and if a Court is a common home of all the realm, it would be fitting that whatever is of such a character as to be common to all without being peculiar to any should frequent this court and dwell there: nor is there any other abode worthy of so great an inmate. Such in fact seems to be that Vulgar Tongue of which we are speaking; and hence it is that those who frequent all the royal palaces always speak the Illustrious Vulgar Tongue. Hence also it happens that our Illustrious Language wanders about like a Wayfarer, and is welcomed in humble shelters, seeing we have no court.

Dante's second book of *On the Vulgar Tongue* deals with poetry as the first book dealt with language. It, too, is important. He says that there are three subjects good enough for the illustrious vernacular. They are *Salus, Venus, Virtus,* that is to say safety (of the state), love, and virtue. Here he does not slavishly follow the ancients or the church fathers. He is speaking of the actual subjects of Romance literature. The Romans and Greeks wrote much about arms, a good deal about virtue (but not in Dante's Christian sense), and little or nothing about love the way Dante understands it. Yet, this new subject is boldly put by Dante on an equal footing with the other two. No doubt much of Dante's "modernity" results from his relative ignorance of classical literature, but it puts him nearer to us in many ways than the more learned critics of the Renaissance.

Nor does this forward-looking book stop here. The best poetic form to use is that of the *canzone,* which contains the best of modern literature. It should be written in the "tragic style" of the illustrious vernacular.

Dante then goes on to a discussion of style and individual words and says many excellent things which are, however, of interest mainly to Italian poets and readers and which cannot be translated into English.

Even though the third and fourth books Dante promised us are lost, what we have is enough to enable us to appreciate his originality. His *De vulgari eloquentia* largely disregarded the question of genres which so dominated classical criticism and concerned itself with language and style, the main interest of modern poets. It gave the highest place to the new subjects the Middle Ages had introduced into literature and praised above all forms the *canzone,* a lyric poem. And when today we think of poetry we, like Dante, think of the lyric before we think of the dramatic or narrative forms, tragedy and the epic. In several ways, then, Dante was the first modern critic.

BIBLIOGRAPHY

Baldwin, C. S. *Medieval Rhetoric and Poetic*. New York, 1928.
Dante. *A Translation of Dante's Eleven Letters* by C. S.
　　Latham. Boston and New York, 1891.
―――. *Epistolae*; tr. by Paget Toynbee. Oxford, 1920.
―――. *A Translation of the Latin Works of Dante Alighieri*.
　　London, 1904.
―――. *De vulgari eloquentia: Commentato da Aristide Marigo*.
　　Florence, 1938.
Dinsmore, C. A. *Aids to the Study of Dante*. Boston and New
　　York, 1903.
Dunbar, H. F. *Symbolism in Medieval Thought*. New Haven,
　　1929.
Grandgent, C. H. *Dante*. New York, 1921.

6 · *Boccaccio* (1313–1375)

SOMETHING HAPPENS between Dante and Boccaccio—a stirring of men's spirits, a renewed interest in classical culture as something worthwhile for its own sake. There is, above all, a consciousness that there are new ways of looking at the world.

Dante reposed securely in what was already an ancient tradition. He did not have to argue the fact that his poetry fitted into this tradition. He accepted his age and knew that his age accepted his poetry. Not so Boccaccio. He feels called upon to defend poetry, not only his own, but all imaginative literature. Dante could concern himself seriously with the details of composition. Boccaccio must look, as did the ancients, at poetry as a whole. His consciousness that poetry may be attacked or defended as a whole is one of the signs that a new age is coming into being.

In his *Life of Dante*, Boccaccio feels he must show that poetry is really theology in order to free it from attacks by theologians. He argues that the ancient poets who wrote the Bible were inspired by the Holy Ghost, who used them to reveal his secrets. In this sense the Holy Ghost himself was a poet.

The Bible is poetry in exactly the same way the profane writings are. It uses allegory and tells stories that have both an obvious and a hidden sense. There is, for example, the story of Nebuchadnezzar's vision. The king saw a statue made of several metals struck down by a rock that changed into a mountain. By this "the Spirit wished to show all succeeding ages that they ought to submit to the doctrine of Christ, who was and is the living rock, and that the Christian religion born of this rock would become a thing immovable and eternal, as we see that the mountains are."

The ancients wrote in the same way. "When they feigned that Saturn had many children and devoured all but four of them, they wished to have understood from this picture nothing else than that Saturn is time, in which everything is produced, and as everything is produced in time, it likewise is the destroyer of all and reduces all to nothing." Thus, in the way they work, poetry and the Scriptures are the same. Since theology is the poetry of God, poetry is theology.

Boccaccio's major defense of poetry is found in his *Genealogy of the Gentile Gods*. In this work, meant to serve as a handbook for poets and the readers of poetry, he searches out and co-ordinates the myths of the ancients. Yet, realizing that the stories of heathen gods might offend the pious, he feels constrained to write a defense of the pagan myths. In the fourteenth and fifteenth books, by defending these myths, he upholds most imaginative literature.

Poetry has strong enemies. First, of course, are the completely carnal men whose minds never rise above the pleasures of the table and the brothel. "Why waste your time with poetry when you can love, sleep, and drink?" they ask. Second are those with a smattering of philosophy who, without ever having come nearer to learning than popular digests, fancy themselves great theologians and scorn the poets as being mere triflers. The third class is composed of the real philistines of this time, the lawyers. They have learning, to be sure, but their learning is entirely for the purpose of gaining money. They hold that any study which keeps its practitioners poor is contemptible. How ridiculous to be a poet and go in rags when you can be a lawyer and gain both power and money. These practical people are hardly worth arguing with. Poets long for retirement, fame, stillness, and peace; lawyers for noise, gold, clamor, and contention. The fourth class contains the most dangerous enemies of poetry, the narrow-minded theologians. Among them are certain friars and others who make a parade of learning to impress the masses. They contend that "poems are false, obscure, lewd, and replete with absurd and silly tales of pagan gods." They shout that poets are nothing but seducers of men, prompters to crime. They claim it is a sin to read or possess the ancient poets, and they use Plato's authority to support the proposition that poets should be banished from society.

Against these enemies Boccaccio enters the arena. He shows how noble poetry is in its origins and how poets have always been esteemed by the great princes of this world. Augustus was the friend of Vergil. King Frederick and the Prince of Verona protected Dante. Petrarch himself can boast of the patronage of emperors, kings, and popes. Since poetry is noble, it is obviously not written for the ignorant. It is obscure only to the common herd. The learned understand it.

Nor do poets tell lies. Those who say this do not understand the nature of poetry. Such charges are made by people who have not even read Homer and Vergil and Horace. To be sure there are wicked poems such as Ovid's *Art of Love*. It was the writers of these that Plato meant when he spoke of banishing poets. Good poetry is not of this kind. It is inspiration plus learning.

All of these and the other arguments Boccaccio gives are of interest but hardly to the main point. His clerical opponents realized that what Boccaccio was doing in this very book as well as in other works was paganizing European literature. He answers this major objection by saying that the pagan poets may have been dangerous in the days when the old gods still had followers but are not today. Christianity is so strongly implanted in men's minds that no danger exists. To be sure, young and callow minds might come to harm, but Boccaccio is writing for mature Christians like himself. To escape all suspicion that he might be unorthodox, he makes it clear that he believes in the major tenets of the Christian faith.

His most important point, though, is the same one he made in his *Life of Dante:* The ancient poets are teachers. The truths they write about are written in allegorical form in the same manner as the stories in the Bible. The world needs what the Greeks and Romans can teach.

Thus, though he uses the old arguments of his predecessors and insists, as Dante did, that poetry is theology, he is actually asking for the freedom of the poet to choose any subject matter he wishes. Offering the classical world to his own, he becomes a prophet of that new world which is going to result from the mixture of the old and the new.

BIBLIOGRAPHY

Boccaccio, Giovanni. *Vita di Dante*. Bari, 1918.
Osgood, C. G. *Boccaccio on Poetry*. Princeton, 1930.
Smith, J. R. *The Earliest Lives of Dante*. New Haven, 1901.
Traversari, Guido. *Scritti intorno al Boccaccio*. Città di Castello, 1907.

7 · The Renaissance Critics (Sixteenth Century)

ONCE THE BARRIERS which Boccaccio labored to weaken were down, a horde of literary critics rushed onto the scene. There was no Longinus or Dante among them, towering above the others. Some wrote better, were more famous, and more influential than others, but few desired, for reasons we shall see later, to be eccentric or original to a degree that would put them apart from their fellows. We can, then, treat them as a group without violating history or their own principles.

In the most important matters they were in agreement. Looking upon the Middle Ages as a semibarbaric period, they were out to bestow form, classical form, on the literature and life of their age. But before they could do so a question of major importance had to be answered. In which language should the new literature be written? It takes a feat of the historical imagination to realize how important this question was. We today would have no hesitation in advising a writer to use the language he learned at his mother's knee. The Renaissance critics could not answer so glibly. Being products of the revival of learning, they could not but feel an almost holy reverence for the languages of Homer and Cicero. Indeed, the situation was seemingly less favorable for the modern languages than it had been in Dante's time. His dream of a unified peninsula under the Holy Roman Emperor had almost faded from Italy. Further, the humanists of the fourteenth century had given to Latin the weight of their great authority. It was no longer merely the more or less corrupt language of the church writers. It was the language of great literature and noble thoughts. From the four-

31

teenth to well into the seventeenth century, a considerable proportion of those who wanted the glory of being read by posterity felt that Latin was a better bet than their native tongue.

A popular humanist theory insisted that the modern dialects were the descendants of the plebeian speech of ancient Rome and that the ancient writers had used a superior language. Thus for moderns to write in "Italian" would be, they contended, as if Cicero and Vergil had written in the speech of the lower classes of Rome. This theory, by the way, has had a long life. People still speak of "vulgar Latin" without being able to produce convincing examples of it. Until they discover some we can doubt whether the popular language of Rome differed any more from written Latin than the slang of our own day does from written English.

The humanists were, of course, actually convinced that Latin was the better literary instrument. No doubt, too, they prided themselves on their difficult achievement and were hesitant in opening their learning to anyone who could speak only his native language.

Fortunately, though, the moderns had on their side three great writers. Dante, Petrarch, and Boccaccio had written in the vernacular. No finespun theories could make men forget this. So it was in Florence, the common home of all three, that the fight for the vernacular was most vigorously waged. Surrounded by despotic states, Florence long remained a Republic. Liberal and republican influences were stronger there than anywhere else in Italy. So, for this reason too, we are not surprised to find Florence at the head of the movement to make the language of the people respectable.

Men like Leon Battista Alberti argued that one should write in a language that all can understand which, if it is not as polished as Latin, will become so if patriots give their attention to it. Then Pietro Bembo, a famous Latinist himself, came over to the side of Florentines and wrote in a vernacular so polished that the old objections could no longer be taken seriously. In a tract written in defense of the vernacular, he argued that a modern language is actually superior to an ancient one for the treatment of modern subjects. Other Florentines added to the demand that the language they spoke be accepted as a literary instrument, and they echoed Bembo's argument that it was patriotic to write in it.

But Italy was not a nation, and this defense of the Florentine vernacular aroused the opposition of those not fortunate enough to have drunk of the Arno. Opposed to Latin, they were equally opposed to having Florentine (or Tuscan) as the literary language. They claimed that they wrote in Italian and demanded that the language be called by that name. They were supported by men like Il Calmeta and Castiglione, both of whom argued that the speech the great church or lay lords used, the "courtier's tongue," was the real national language. They borrowed many of Dante's arguments from his *De vulgari eloquentia* to support their cause.

Actually, though, all of these people wrote in a more or less modified Florentine, whether they called it Italian or the courtier's tongue. The question was argued right up through the nineteenth century. The eventual compromise, still in existence today, was to write in Florentine and call it Italian.

In England and France the problem of the language was less difficult. Both were unified monarchies, and there was no question of strongly competing dialects. Both countries, however, had the Latin tradition to overcome, and the writers in both countries made good use of the arguments of their Italian predecessors.

The fighters for French and English had, as their Italian fellows had not, the support of strong Protestant movements. The publication of the Scriptures in translation was probably the greatest single force in establishing the victory of the vernacular. Tyndale, who paid for his translation with his life, taunts an opponent with these words: "If God spare my life, ere many years I will cause a boy that draweth the plow shall know more of the scriptures than thou dost."

In both England and France, growing nationalism helped forward the victory. Du Bellay's *Defense and Illustration of the French Language* (1549) appeals openly to nationalistic sentiments. The French are as good as the Romans or any other people, ancient or modern, and there is no reason why they shouldn't use their own language. It is the patriotic duty of all French scholars to write in French and to enrich it with their learning, declared Du Bellay and his followers. That so many Frenchmen urged the language be enriched shows they were quite conscious that French was not yet the perfect language. They spurred on writers to borrow or steal terms from other languages so as to give French a richer vocabulary.

The English were, if possible, even more patriotic. For hundreds of years the court and the nobility had spoken French. Though by Renaissance times English had been re-established, a strong tradition of hostility to foreign linguistic domination had taken root. Yet the English tongue of the early Renaissance must have seemed a crude thing to the learned men of letters. When Ascham writes his *Toxophilus* (1545) in English he confesses "to have written this book either in Latin or Greek . . . had been more easier." Bacon, conscious of how the language had changed since Chaucer's day, had his *Essays* put into Latin because "these modern languages will at one time or other play bankrupt with books."

The patriotic writers won the day. Mulcaster claimed that English was the "joyful title of our liberty and freedom, the Latin tongue remembering us of our thraldom and bondage." Others urged that English be enriched by borrowing and trans-lation, while inconsistently declaring that English was superior to all other tongues.

In both France and England the standard chosen was, as might be imagined from the social structure of the age, that of the upper classes. In England the popular catchword, "the King's English" tells us all we need to know. For the purposes of actual writing, though, three styles were recognized—the high, the middle, and the low, a division which roughly followed that of the main social groupings.

The circumstance that the opening of learning to the people by the use of the vernacular can, and often does, lead to political democracy should not blind us to the fact that the Renaissance was a strongly aristocratic age. The very men who could argue for the use of the language of the people had nothing but scorn for the people themselves. This is not surprising in itself—the French Revolution and the Rights of Man were far in the future—but the effect of this scorn on their critical principles was great. The Renaissance raised snobbishness almost to the position of an esthetic.

In one of his odes, Horace said, *Odi profanum vulgus* ("I hate the profane mob"). This phrase was inscribed on the banners of almost every critic of the Renaissance. Petrarch declared that the praise of the mob is odious to the learned. Bembo bluntly stated that the people cannot tell good literature from bad. Others condemned the popular romances of the day simply because they were popular. Men like Ariosto and Tasso were condemned because they were widely read and sung. The speech of the poet should, they declared, be far removed from the speech of the market place. Since the people were pleased by rhyme, some learned critics began advocating that Italian verse be written in rhymeless hexameter after the fashion of the Romans. Since in Italian it was almost impossible not to rhyme, such a suggestion was indeed a heroic attempt to flee the mob.

The French take up the cry *Odi profanum vulgus*. Du Bellay, in a preface to *L'Olive* (1549), declares that a select handful of readers is all he desires. "I do not, at all," he says, "want popular applause." One of his contemporaries, Le Caron, claims that the secret of poetry is obscurity. He insists that the greatest pleasure in the world is to discover things as far removed as possible from the knowledge of the vulgar. Thus he can declare that poets, "thinking it unworthy to prostitute their secret inventions to the profane mob, have covered them with fables so as to be understood only by the wise and learned." Ronsard looks at the matter from the linguistic point of view. The French language is poor because it is the language of the people. The duty of the poet is to find rich and precious words to ennoble it, "regardless of how people murmur." Though the abolition of rhyme and the introduction of classical quantities is contrary to the nature of the language, Jacques de la Taille gets over this difficulty by changing the spelling and pronunciation of French.

England follows right along. In Spenser's *Teares of the Muses*, Polyhymnia, while happy that Queen Elizabeth and a select circle can appreciate poetry, adds:

But all the rest as born of savage brood,
And having been with acorns always fed,
Can no whit favor this celestial food,
But with base thoughts are into blindness led,
And kept from looking on the lightsome day:
For whom I wail and weep all that I may.

Rhyme is condemned by some as being the invention of the Goths and Huns. Protestant bias enters in, too. The Middle Ages were Catholic, so rhyme is considered on a par with Popery. Puttenham calls rhyme, "the idle invention of monastical men," and adds, "Thus what in writing of rimes and registring of lies was the clergy of that fabulous age wholly occupied." The greatest objection to rhyme, however, is that it is popular. If classical meters were used, says Puttenham, "surely then rash ignorant heads, which now can easily reckon up fourteen syllables, and easily stumble on every rime, either durst not, for lack of such learning, or else would not, in avoiding such labor, be so busy as everywhere they be, and shops in London should not be so full of lewd and rude rimes, as commonly they are."

One should go back to the ancients even for meter. Here we have a good example of what the Renaissance meant by *imitation*. Imitation for Plato and Aristotle was the imitation of persons and things in nature. Horace and Longinus begin to use it as meaning the imitation of other writers. This latter sense is the one in which it was most often used by the Renaissance critics.

Since they regarded the age that had preceded them as crude and formless, they looked for form to the Greeks and Romans. However, it was more often to the Roman Empire rather than to the democracies of Greece that their eyes turned. This was partly because Rome offered the prototype of the society they most admired. They loved Vergil because he had, in a sense, created a new literature for a new empire. The Greeks were more foreign. Homer was not civilized enough; Giraldi Cinthio condemned Homer for allowing a princess, Nausicaä, to wash clothes and explained this lack of taste by reminding his readers that Homer wrote before the majesty and excellence of the Roman Empire came into being. Spenser translated into Eng-

lish a sonnet of Du Bellay's which shows the hold that Rome
had on men's imaginations:

> Such as the Berecynthian Goddess bright
> In her swift charret with high turrets crown'd,
> Proud that so many Gods she brought to light;
> Such was this City in her good days found:
> This City, more than that great Phrygian mother
> Renown'd for fruit of famous progeny,
> Whose greatness by the greatness of none other,
> But by her self, her equal match could see.
> Rome only might to Rome compared be,
> And only Rome could make great Rome to tremble:
> So did the Gods by heavenly doom decree,
> That other earthly power should not resemble
> Her that did match the whole earth's puissance,
> And did her courage to the heavens advance.

It was the spirit of Rome, not only Roman forms, which the
writers wanted to imitate, but they were not conscious of any
strong distinction between the two. They felt that to write in
the ancient forms or genres of epic, tragedy, and comedy, to
mold their style upon that of the great ancients, was the best
way of attaining to the ancient spirit.

The desire for form extended throughout life. At this time
many of our own conceptions of "polite society" came into being. It was an age of books on how to be a courtier and a
gentleman. Men were made conscious that there are rules of
behavior, a decorum, one should follow. What was considered
fitting or decorous for life was so considered for literature. The
Italian critic Daniello termed decorum the special study of
the poet.

One could look at almost all of Renaissance criticism in terms
of this word alone. Genres are classified according to the class
of people they deal with; style is considered largely a matter of
seeing that people speak as their position in society demands
that they speak. Scaliger divides style into the grand, the middle, and the humble, and tells us that the high style is to be
used for "gods, heroes, kings, and generals, and not for inferior
characters such as sailors, hostlers, and tradesmen." Ronsard
even divides the alphabet into noble and less noble letters. If the
poet would keep decorum, he must not only use the right style

for each character but also describe actions differently according to the class of the person acting. As Puttenham writes:

> In speaking or writing of a Prince's affairs and fortunes there is a certain *Decorum,* that we may not use the same terms in their business as we might very well do in a meaner person's, the case being all one, such reverence is due to their estates. As for example, if an Historiographer shall write of an Emperor or King, how such a day he joined battle with his enemy, and being over-laid ran out of the field, and took to his heels, or put spur to his horse, and fled as fast as he could, the terms be not decent; but of a mean soldier or captain it was not undecently spoken.

This desire for social and moral stereotypes is strengthened by the feeling that this is what Aristotle meant when he said that poetry dealt with universals. Horace's remarks about portraying young men as wild, old men as avaricious, and so forth, fitted in beautifully with their taste.

Quite naturally, the Renaissance critics apply social criteria to their discussion of the genres of literature. Recognizing that society is divided into classes and discovering from Aristotle and the practice of Greek dramatists that the characters of tragedy and comedy are of different social classes, they make the rank of the characters the distinguishing difference between the dramatic genres.

Tragedy is ranked highest among plays because its characters are kings and princes, as well as because Aristotle's *Poetics* discussed this genre most fully. The plot is based upon the activities of kings—the affairs of state, fortress, and camp—says Scaliger. Giraldi Cinthio says that we call the actions of tragedy illustrious, not because they are virtuous but because the characters who act are of the highest rank. The style of writing employed must be the highest, since any lower would be unworthy of kings and princes. In Italy, especially, the stage scenery was considered important and it was ordered that magnificent palaces should serve as a background for the action.

Comedy deals with people of the middle class. Obviously the plots must be suitable to such persons and to the middle-class customs with which the poets are familiar. Minturno suggests that although noble ladies appear in public, middle-class girls do not until marriage, and that the poet will violate decorum if he has them do so on the stage. Castelvetro declares that members of the strong-willed aristocracy constitute a law unto themselves but the middle-class persons of comedy are poor in heart, run to magistrates with their troubles, and live under the law. Thus the plots of comedies must not contain vendettas or other actions unsuitable to the characters but must be drawn from bourgeois and private life. The speech must be the everyday speech in the middle style between the high and the low.

There is one dramatic form reserved for the lowest classes. It is the farce. Here the language is that of the gutter and the actions are appropriately low.

The French and English critics follow this threefold division and give almost word for word the same definitions as do the Italians. For instance, Laudun sums up the matter for the French as follows: "The characters of Tragedy are grave people of great rank and those of Comedy are low and of small position. . . . The words of Tragedy are grave and those of Comedy are light. . . . The characters in Tragedy are sumptuously dressed and those of Comedy garbed in an ordinary way."

Many similar quotations could be given from the English critics if there were need. Even the practicing dramatists did much the same thing. Most of Shakespeare's tragedies and comedies roughly fit into the main distinctions as to rank, action, and language. Ben Jonson, realizing he had not kept the unity of time, felt that it was unimportant in comparison with these other things. He said in his preface to *Sejanus*: "First, if it be objected, that what I publish is no true poem, in the strict laws of time, I confess it. . . . In the meantime, if in truth of argument, dignity of person, gravity and height of elocution, fullness and frequency of sentence, I have discharged the other offices of a tragic writer, let not the absence of these forms be imputed to mè."

Yet the English critics were not satisfied that the playwrights kept strict-enough decorum. Many of the dramatists wrote plays in which the class of characters, speech, and action were all mixed up. George Whetstone said that they made clowns companions to kings and used "one order of speech for all persons; a gross *Indecorum*." A famous passage in Sir Philip

Sidney's *Apology for Poetry* registered the same complaint: "All their plays be neither right tragedies nor right comedies; mingling kings and clowns, not because the matter so carrieth it, but thrust in the clown by head and shoulders, to play a part in majestical matters, with neither decency nor discretion: So as neither the admiration and commiseration, nor the right sportfulness, is by their mongrel tragi-comedy obtained." Obviously, to Sidney, as to other conservatives, a tragicomedy was no true genre. On the other hand, a somewhat later writer, John Fletcher, wrote a tragicomedy and defended it: "A God," he says, "is as lawful in this as in a tragedy, and mean people as in a comedy."

Naturally, Fletcher knew of the bitter discussion that had taken place in Italy on this question. A critic named De Nores had written that mixed genres were not even worthy of discussion. Guarini, the author of *Il pastor fido*, however, sprang to the defense of his own practice. He argued that since the great and the lowly exist side by side in every country, it is perfectly correct to have both in a drama. De Nores answered that comedy instructs citizens on how to act. Then he asked a series of questions. How can you keep decorum if the characters are of different rank? What level of language are you going to use, the grand or humble? Are the stage settings going to be palaces or humble cottages? He answered his questions by saying that whatever you did would be inappropriate for one class of your characters.

Guarini was afraid to answer merely by saying that he wrote to please, though he hinted at it. No, he too had to use the standard social arguments. He said that a pastoral tragicomedy like his *Il pastor fido* was an acceptable genre because some of the shepherds were noble and others were not. The first made for the tragedy, the second for the comedy. The two together made tragicomedy. Guarini added pastoral to his definition to show that the characters were shepherds.

Another critic, Faustino Summo, jumped into the fray, looked at the whole argument from the viewpoint of decorum, and decided that De Nores was right and Guarini was wrong. Mixed genres violate decorum and that's that. The fact that *Il pastor fido* was a melodious and charming poem seems not even to have entered into the discussion.

There is relatively little theorizing about lyric poetry and the minor forms during the Renaissance. They are much harder to discuss in the social terms the critics felt at ease with. Not so the epic. It comes in for a full share of attention.

We have seen a nationalistic strain in the fight for the vernacular and an aristocratic one in the consideration of the genres. In the criticism on the epic they merge, particularly in France and England.

The Italian critics maintain that an epic should deal with the adventures of a great hero, usually a legitimate prince seeking his heritage. Though unlike a tragedy in that people of different ranks appear, the form is a noble one since the protagonist is of royal rank. But since, of necessity, many characters appear, the poet must take care to see that decorum is kept for all the ranks introduced. These critics give little emphasis to the epic's national qualities. The long poems of Ariosto and others make the French Roland their hero.

The French critics, much more nationalistic, are particularly anxious that a French poet present France with a great epic. Du Bellay in his *Defense and Illustration* claims that France needs a great epic to spread the fame of its language as Vergil's *Aeneid* did that of Rome. He promises the French poet who will undertake such a task everlasting glory and the gratitude of his countrymen. His friend, Pierre de Ronsard, hearkens to these promises and writes *La Franciade* (1572).

In England a number of poets aspired to become the English Vergil. Spenser, Warner, and Drayton all write long poems glorifying the nation. Partly because it can celebrate the nation, the epic, or heroic poem, is placed above tragedy by William Webbe and Sir Philip Sidney. To the first it is "verily and incomparably the best of all other." The second writes: "If anything be already said in the defense of sweet poetry, all concurreth to the maintaining of the Heroical, which is not only a kind, but the best and most accomplished kind of poetry."

The epic should, the critics agree, be based on history, preferably national history. Spenser's *Faerie Queene* is written to glorify Elizabeth and England, yet the action is put in the past in order to remove the danger of controversy that a modern theme would arouse. Spenser says, "I chose the history of King Arthur, as most fit for the excellency of his person, being made famous by many men's former works, and also furthest from the danger of envy, and suspicion of present time. In which I have followed all the antique poets historical."

A problem connected with the epic appeared in Italy. Were the long verse romances of Boiardo, Ariosto, and Tasso to be considered epics? Although these poems had their defenders, and certain critics considered the romance as the modern form of the epic, many condemned them because, being popular with the people, they were unworthy of consideration by learned critics. When someone speaks of the romances as being eagerly sung by many, Minturno replies: "True, but by whom, and of what judgment? Certainly by vulgar men that do not know what poetry is, nor in what the excellence of the poet consists."

The French critics are not greatly concerned with this problem, but the English are. The romances in England belonged to the past and the past was Roman Catholic. Thus Protestant feeling was added to the scorn the critics felt anyway for the productions of the "Dark Ages." The medieval romances are roundly condemned. Ascham's attitude in the *Scholemaster* is typical:

> In our forefather's time, when Papistry, as a standing pool, covered and overflowed all England, few books were read in our tongue, saving certain books of chivalry, as they said, for pastime and pleasure, which, as some say, were made in monasteries, by idle Monks or wanton Canons: as one for example, *Morte Arthure*, the whole pleasure of which book standeth in two special points, in open manslaughter and bold baudry. In which book those be counted the noblest Knights that do kill most men without any quarrel, and commit foulest adulteries by subtlist shifts.

An additional reason is found for avoiding the old romances. As more sophisticated readers turn to the new poetry, the common people still cherish the old romances. This in itself is enough to condemn them. Beaumont and Fletcher's play *The Knight of the Burning Pestle* satirizes from the courtly point of view the taste of the plain people for the romances and the tradesman's delight in picturing himself and his apprentices as heroic figures.

The medieval prejudice against poetry and against poets as mere jesters or entertainers still existed in some quarters during this period. No doubt that is why the literary critics feel called upon, not only to defend poetry as Boccaccio had done, but to protect the poet himself against adverse criticism. First they point to the poetry in the Bible, inspired by the Holy Spirit, and conclude that the poet is like the holy prophets. Then they borrow Plato's theory that the poet is inspired by God and this, in their opinion, elevates him above most mortal men. Indeed, is he, they ask, not like God himself since like God he creates?

Earthly honors are the poets', too. The critics boast of the kings and potentates who have honored poets with their patronage. The very system of patronage that linked the poets with the nobles and the courts made them anxious to ennoble the profession of poetry so that it would not be looked down upon as inferior to hunting and war and other noble pastimes.

Yet side by side with the claim that the poet is honored above all men is the fact that the aristocrat is often reluctant to publish his verse. Puttenham writes: "I know very many noble Gentlemen in the court that have written commendably and suppressed it again, or else suffered it to be published without their own names to it; as if it were a discredit for a Gentleman to seem learned and to show himself amorous of any good Art." Even Sir Philip Sidney, who claims all glories for the makers of poetry, can say, "I know not by what mischance in these my not old years and idlest times [I have] slipt into the title of a Poet."

This is part of that air of effortless grace which the well-bred man assumes in all things. The harder the poet has worked over his poems, the more he should pretend that they are trifles he has dashed off for lack of something better to do.

Some of the poets and critics are of gentle birth and are not slow to let their readers know it. Some go so far as to claim that, since poetry is the noble science par excellence, base birth disqualifies a man for the profession of poetry. As Spenser says in the *Shepherd's Calendar*:

> O peerless Poesy, where is then thy place?
> If nor in Prince's palace thou do sit:
> (And yet is Prince's palace the most fit)
> Ne breast of baser birth doth thee embrace.

Or, to quote Spenser again, since he puts in pleasing verse what the other critics are saying in prose, the need of the day is to take poetry away from the common people and put it back in the hands of the nobles:

> Whilom in ages past none might profess
> But Princes and high Priests that secret skill,
> The sacred laws therein they won't express,
> And with deep Oracles their verses fill:
> Then was she held in sovereign dignity,
> And made the nursling of Nobility.

> But now nor Prince nor Priest does her maintain,
> But suffer her prophaned for to be
> Of the base vulgar, that with hands unclean
> Dares to pollute her hidden mystery.
> And treadeth under foot her holy things,
> Which was the care of Caesars and of Kings.

But learning as well as gentle blood is necessary. The French critics have great contempt for the mere "courtier poet" who caters to the less sophisticated tastes that exist even in the courts. One must know his classics in order to imitate the ancients. The poet is the teacher of the age and must know all. Scaliger, who is a physician, a physicist, a botanist, and a grammarian as well as a poet and literary critic, insists that no learning is foreign to the muses. Gabriel Harvey writes: "It is not sufficient for poets to be superficial humanists; they must be exquisite artists and universal scholars." The ideal poet is a Leonardo da Vinci who takes all knowledge for his province.

The poet must know all so that he can teach all. The Renaissance critics are not of the "art for art's sake" school. They believe in the pedagogical theory of art. Horace had said that poetry either teaches or delights. Scaliger gives the prevailing Renaissance version of this when he states that poetry teaches delightfully. This is in answer to the medieval view that poetry is either dangerous or a waste of time.

The critics are also conscious of Plato's protest against poetry. Scaliger claims that Homer is a better teacher than many philosophers and that no poem is as full of bad things as Plato's own *Republic*. Tassoni lists poetry as one of the three arts necessary for the well-being of the state. The first is history, which teaches the rulers, the second is poetry, which teaches the people, and the third is oratory, which teaches lawyers how to defend cases. De Nores says that poetry purges the citizens of dangerous emotions, makes them content with the government under which they live, and helps to train young men for the state militia.

Each of the genres has its own teaching function. Tragedy, dealing with kings, seems ideally designed for an audience of one—the ruler. The critics agree that the purpose of tragedy is to present terrifying accidents that may befall the great in order that princes may learn to moderate their ambitions. De Nores suggests that its function for the people is, by showing the horror of tyranny, to make them content with the well-ordered monarchy under which they live. But though all people can, no doubt, learn from the errors of princes, the first English classical tragedy, *Gorboduc*, was written to teach a lesson to a single person, Queen Elizabeth.

The purpose of comedy is to teach the common people to avoid the follies incident of their way of life. Mazzoni says that since comedies end happily they console the plebeians for their low station in life. De Nores feels that turbulence and discontent are allayed by comedy, which makes people love private life and the state under which they live.

The epic, of course, has a patriotic purpose, but it has an aristocratic one, too. It is the poetic form of the courtier's book, which teaches noblemen how to act properly. The epic teaches them the virtues of their class, particularly the warlike ones. The picture of the epic hero, says Sidney, stirs the mind with a desire to be like him and counsels how to be worthy. Spenser tells us clearly the function of his *Faerie Queene*. He writes:

The general end therefore of all the book is to fashion a gentleman or noble person in virtuous and gentle discipline. Which for that I conceived should be most plausible and pleasing being colored with an historical fiction—the which the most part of men delight to read rather for variety of matter than for profit of the ensample— I chose the history of King Arthur. . . .

This is a clear statement of the "sugar-coated pill" theory of
literature. Most men would rather be entertained than taught.
The poet uses his poetic devices in order to make people read
him. He attempts to inculcate not only "glory" but all the other
virtues needed to fashion a gentleman.

Another obvious function of poetry, particularly of the lyric
genres, is to praise the poet's patron. One of the defenses of
poetry most often cited is that it gives everlasting fame to great
men. Who would know of the deeds of Achilles and Aeneas
if it had not been for Homer and Vergil? Great men who want
their fame to last longer than marble and bronze are as much
dependent on the poets as the poets are on them for patronage.

In presenting this synthetic view of Renaissance criticism,
we have been unable to do justice to each and every critic.
Sidney, for instance, although the main pattern of his ideas was
traditional, does give the reader the feeling that he was a man
whose heart as well as his head responded to literature. In a
flash of independence he could write of the *Ballad of Chevy
Chase* in these words:"Certainly, I must confess my own bar-
barousness: I never heard the old song of Percy and Douglas
that I found not my heart moved more than with a trumpet;
and yet it is sung by some blind crowder, with no rougher voice
than rude style. . . ." Such passages are few, however, and
Sidney like his fellows seldom departs from the main line of
Renaissance critical thought.

One critic, however, dared to be different. He was that
Lodovico Castelvetro, who translated and annotated the *Poetics*
of Aristotle in the last half of the sixteenth century. Castelvetro
asserts his independence by denying emphatically that the poet
is inspired by divine furor. This opinion, he says, originated in
the ignorance of the mob and has been kept alive by the vain-
glory of the poets themselves.

An even more striking departure from accepted doctrine is
his blunt denial that poetry teaches. Science and history seek
truth, but the end of poetry is pleasure, not teaching. This being so, tragedy is superior to epic because it delights the
audience more, an audience which for him is not a group of
courtly aristocrats but the *moltitudine rozza*, the rude mob.

Nor will he allow learning in poetry. Anything which the people cannot understand has no place. Even ideas should be limited to those the people already accept. His theory is one that many television producers must hold.

Since an unsophisticated audience is easily impressed by the labor involved in a work of art (a picture that the guide says took twenty years to paint will always draw "ohs" and "ahs" from the tourists), he makes the "difficulty overcome" one of the criteria of art. Since to copy from another does not involve any labor, the ancients should not be imitated. The marvellous is the basis of artistic pleasure since this is what most pleases the mass audience.

With all his originality, Castelvetro was a man with the viewpoint of his age. One who calls the people the "crude mob" is no democrat. He accepted the class divisions of the dramatic genres and was in addition as much a rulemaker as his brother critics. It was he who formulated the unities of time and space which are often considered to be the very hallmark of pseudo-classicism.

Yet he was an original mind in an age when originality was dangerous. Though this had nothing to do with his critical theories, he was arrested by the Inquisition, escaped by night, and fled out of Italy. He wrote his great book in exile. The first edition was put on the *Index of Prohibited Books* and all copies were burned. The second, carefully revised by a friend, met slightly better luck. It was merely required that it be expurgated before being considered safe. As a result most copies one comes across have numerous passages carefully crossed out in ink. But time has played a trick on the censors. The ink has faded. Now all the "heretical" passages are easily read.

There is usually a gap between the dry bones of critical theory and the living productions of poets and playwrights. It used to be fashionable to say that although the criticism of the Renaissance was "classic," the practice was "romantic." The plays of Shakespeare are so much more than the critical doctrines of his time that this view has a surface plausibility. The difference, however, has been exaggerated by equating Renaissance with neoclassical criticism, although they are not the same. Most Renaissance literature can fit roughly into the pattern that the

Renaissance critics lay down. Even Shakespeare's plays keep in large measure the decorum that is at the basis of his age's criticism, though not as strictly as Sidney would have desired. One could easily show how Shakespeare's tragedies deal with kings and have the appropriate plot and diction, his comedies with private affairs and the like. Even his so-called mixture of genres could find defense in such critics as Guarini.

The actual creators of literature had less trouble defending their productions according to prevailing critical standards than we might at first assume. Tasso's great romance is successfully presented (as a modern epic) by the poet in his *Discourses on the Heroic Poem*. He claims the right to use Christian and modern subjects instead of pagan and ancient ones and realizes that at least some of the critics will support him.

Only occasionally does a writer admit that his works cannot be defended critically. Such a one, however, is the great Spanish playwright Lope de Vega. In his *New Art of Making Comedies* he carefully gives the rules for comedy according to the best practice of the ancients and the theories of the Italian critics. Then he confesses that contemporary Spanish taste has not allowed him to write his own plays according to these rules. He writes, he says, in a "barbarous manner" since that is what his audience demands. The crowd pays the bills and the playwright must write "stupidly" in order to please it. He knows that the theorists of Italy and France call him ignorant and say that of his four hundred and eighty-three comedies all but six sin grievously against art. And he is forced to agree with the critics. His only defense is that if he had written more correctly his plays would have pleased fewer people.

The great glory of the Renaissance critics remains. With all their faults they set the standards for their own age and the age that followed them. If their criticism was more restrictive than inspirational, it must be recognized that their contemporaries were more likely to err on the side of license than that of restraint. But regardless of whether their influence was good or bad they succeeded admirably in doing one thing. They established literary criticism as an independent form of literature. Henceforth the critic was given an honorable place as a citizen in the republic of letters.

BIBLIOGRAPHY

Alberti, L. B. *Opere volgari*. Florence, 1825.

Ascham, Roger. *English Works: Toxophilus; Report of the Affaires and State of Germany; The Scholemaster*; ed by W. A. Wright. Cambridge, 1904.

Atkins, John W. H. *English Literary Criticism: The Renascence*. 2nd ed. London, 1951.

Baïf, J. A. de. *Œuvres en rime*; ed. by Marty-Laveau. 5 vols. Paris, 1881–1890.

Baldwin, C. S. *Renaissance Literary Theory and Practice*; ed. with introd. by D. L. Clark. New York, 1939.

Bembo, Pietro. *Prose scelte; con prefazione di Francesco Coster*. Milan, 1880.

Buck, August. *Italienische Dictungslehren vom Mittelalter bis zum Ausgang der Renaissance*. Tübingen, 1952.

Campion, Thomas. *Songs and Masques with Observations in the Art of English Poesy*; ed. by A. H. Bullen. London, 1903.

Castelvetro, Lodovico. *Opere varie critiche; colla vita dell' autore scritta da L. A. Murator*. Lyons, 1727.

———. *Poetica d'Aristotele vulgarizzata et sposta*. Basel, 1576.

Charlton, H. B. *Castelvetro's Theory of Poetry*. Manchester, 1913

Clements, R. J. *Critical Theory and Practice of the Pléiade*. Cambridge, 1942.

———. *Picta poesis; Literary and Humanistic Theory in Renaissance Emblem Books*. Roma, 1960.

Cook, A. S. *The Art of Poetry: the Poetical Treatises of Horace, Vida and Boileau*. Boston, 1892.

Daniel, Samuel. *Complete Works*; ed. by A. B. Grosart. 5 vols. London, 1885–1896.

Daniello, Bernardino, *La Poetica*. Venice, 1536.

De Nores, Jason. *Apologia contra l'autore del Verato*. Padua, 1590.

Doran, Madeline. *Endeavors of Art: a Study of Form in Elizabethan Drama*. Madison, 1954.

Du Bellay, Joachim. *La Défense et illustration de la langue française;* ed. by Henri Chamard. Paris, 1904.

———. *The Defence and Illustration of the French Language;* tr. by Gladys M. Turquet. London, 1939.

Estienne, Henri. *Deux Dialogues du nouveau langage françois italianisé;* ed. by P. Ristelhuber. 2 vols. Paris, 1885.

Fracastoro, Girolamo. *Naugerius; sive, de poetica dialogus.* Translated by Ruth Kelso. University of Illinois, 1924.

Giraldi Cinthio, Giambattista. *Scritti estetici; de' romanzi, delle comedie e delle tragedie.* 2 vols. Biblioteca rara da Daelli, nos. LI-LII. Milan, 1864.

Guarini, Giambattista. *Opere.* Verona, 1737.

Hall, R. A. Jr. *The Italian questione della lingua.* Chapel Hill, 1942.

Hall, Vernon, Jr. *Life of Julius Caesar Scaliger, 1484–1558.* Transactions of the American Philosophical Society. Philadelphia, 1950.

———. *Renaissance Literary Criticism: A Study of its Social Content.* New York, 1945; reprint, Gloucester, Mass., 1959.

Hathaway, Baxter. *The Age of Criticism: the Late Renaissance in Italy.* Ithaca, New York, 1962.

Herrick, M. T. *The Fusion of Horatian and Artistotelian Literary Criticism.* Urbana, 1946.

Kern, Edith. *The Influence of Hensius and Vossius upon French Dramatic Theory.* Baltimore, 1949.

Kristeller, P. O. *The Philosophy of Marsilio Ficino;* tr. by Virginia Conant. New York, 1943.

La Taille, Jean de. *De l'Art de la tragédie;* ed. by Fred West. Manchester, 1939.

Laudun, Pierre de. *L'Art poétique françois; éd. critique, essai sur la poésie dans le languedoc de Ronsard à Malherbe par J. Dedieu.* Toulouse, 1909.

Minturno, Antonio. *L'Arte poetica del Sig. A. M. nella quale si contengono i precetti heroici, tragici, comici, satyrici, e d'ogni altra poesia.* Venice, 1563.

Padelford, F. M. *Select Translations from Scaliger's Poetics.* New York, 1905.

Patterson, W. F. *Three Centuries of French Poetic Theory.*

University of Michigan Publications of Language and Literature, XIV-XV. Ann Arbor, 1935.

Peletier du Mans, Jacques. *L'Art poétique (1555)*; ed. by A. Boulanger. Paris, 1930.

Scaliger, J. C. *Poetices libri septem*. Lyons, 1561.

Sébillet, Thomas. *L'Art poétique françois*. Paris, 1910.

Smith, G. G., ed. *Elizabethan Essays*. Vols. I and II. Oxford, 1937.

Spingarn, J. E. A *History of Literary Criticism in the Renaissance*. New York, 1908.

———, ed. *Critical Essays of the Seventeenth Century*. 3 vols. Oxford, 1908.

Tasso, Torquato. *Opere*. 6 vols. Florence, 1724.

Trissino, Giangiorgio, and Claudio Tolomei. *Il Castellano di Giangiorgio Trissino ed il Cesano di Claudio Tolomei*. Milan, 1864.

Tuve, Rosemond. *Elizabethan and Metaphysical Imagery; Renaissance Poetic and Twentieth-Century Critics*. Chicago, 1947.

Vida, Marco G. *De Arte poetica*. Cremona, 1527.

Weinberg, Bernard. A *History of Literary Criticism in the Italian Renaissance*. Chicago, 1961.

8 · Milton (1608–1674)

WE HAVE SEEN how the literary criticism of the Renaissance was colored by the social conditions of the age. As social conditions change, we should expect criticism to change too. We can see hints of a different attitude in England because of the revolution of the seventeenth century. King Charles lost his head on the scaffold; the ancient loyalties were shaken to their foundations. The England of the Commonwealth was in some ways a new England with a new set of social and political ideas.

That it is not an age of literary criticism cannot be entirely explained by the fact that the English were too busy building the New Jerusalem. The old criticism, as well as the old literature, was too closely connected with the old order of things to arouse the enthusiasm of the Commonwealth men. When the Parliament issued its edict banning the theater, it acted not only from a Puritan distaste for "poetry" but for political reasons. Not only were the actors and playwrights Royalists for the most part, but the plays they gave often mocked the London middle class, which was the backbone of the Parliament Party in London.

John Milton was for Parliament, was against the King, and was a member of the Commonwealth Government. He was also not only a poet but a serious student of literary criticism. As a result we find in his own criticism (side by side with hints of a new point of view) much that merely repeats what the older critics said.

The old monarchial-aristocratic conception of the poet's function is no longer acceptable. For Milton, poets are the strong

enemies of despotism. Henceforth, the poet must use his gifts
to "inbreed and cherish in a great people the seeds of virtue
and public civility, to allay the perturbations of the mind . . .
to sing the virtuous agonies of martyrs and saints, the deeds and
triumphs of just and pious nations doing valiantly through faith
against the enemies of Christ; to deplore the general relapses of
kingdoms and states from justice and God's true worship." The
poet still teaches, but now he is to teach Milton's love of liberty
and purified religion.

Milton looks to the Bible to furnish his types of poetry, as
his predecessors did to the classics for theirs. The Song of Sol-
omon is a pastoral drama, the Apocalypse of St. John is a high
and stately tragedy, and so forth. When he considers writing
an epic on King Arthur, it is because he may be made the pattern of a *Christian* hero and not because as Spenser saw him
he was "perfected in the twelve private moral virtues as Aristotle
hath devised" or because by portraying him he could "fashion
a gentleman or noble person in virtuous and gentle discipline."

Because of his new political and religious ideas, Milton never
uses the key word decorum in a class sense. For him the meaning is always moral or aesthetic. He accuses an opponent (Sal-
masius) of being ignorant of decorum because he "ascribes to
the vilest men sentiments which could become only the good
and wise."

Though, like the stricter critics before him, Milton is against
the mixing of genres, it is not because of the difference between
kings and subjects. He considers true tragedy not in terms of
kings and princes but in terms of men whose moral worth has
raised them to a high position. His own *Samson Agonistes*,
modelled as it is on ancient tragedy, rejects the distinctions of
birth and social position. The chorus addressed Samson with
these significant words:

> Strongest of mortal men,
> To lowest pitch of abject fortune thou art fall'n.
> For him I reckon not in high estate
> Whom long descent of birth
> Or the sphere of fortune raises;
> But thee whose strength, while vertue was her mate,
> Might have subdu'd the Earth,
> Universally crown'd with highest praises.

The leading characters of tragedy may even be used to point out the errors of princes. He writes: "For a satyr, as it was born out of a tragedy, so ought to resemble his parentage to strike high, and adventure dangerously, at the most eminent vices among the greatest persons." Nor does Milton mean by this merely what the Renaissance critics meant when they said tragedy should teach kings not to be tyrants. Milton wants no kings, tyrants or not.

Since he is interested in both poetry and the Commonwealth, it is natural that he should give advice to the magistrates on the political function of poetry. He agrees with them in their condemnation of "libidinous and ignorant poetasters," but advises them that poetry is necessary to the spirit of man. What the magistrates should do is to encourage the kind of poetry they want. Faced with the role of poetry in the Commonwealth, his attitude for a moment seems to be that of Plato in his Republic. Milton writes:

It were happy for the Commonwealth if our magistrates, as in those famous governments of old, would take into their care not only the deciding of our contentious law cases and brawls, but the managing of our public sports and festival pastimes; that they might not be such as were authorized a while since, the provocations of drunkenness and hurt, but such as may inure and harden our bodies by martial exercises to all warlike skill and performance; and may civilize, adorn, and make discreet our minds by the learned and affable meeting of frequent academies, and the procurement of wise and artful recitations sweetened with eloquent and graceful enticements to the love and practice of justice, temperance, and fortitude, instructing and bettering the nation at all opportunities, that the call of wisdom and virtue may be heard everywhere.

Milton is not Plato, however. This passage is written to convince the magistrates who are suspicious of poetry because of the old theater. Milton himself, as is shown in his *Areopagitica*, would not restrict freedom as Plato would. Milton does feel, however, that the time has come for a more moral and patriotic English poetry. To have this poetry one must have freedom. As a good patriot his hope for poetry lies in an England that is getting rid of the "impertinent yoke of prelaty, under whose inquisitorious and tyrannical duncery no free and splendid wit can flourish."

Being for freedom, Milton, the son of a scrivener, rejects the old class standards for poetry. In their place he emphasizes moral standards. But, in turn, these standards are those of the middle class who are beginning to demand their rights, not those of the ignorant crowd, with whom the learned Milton refuses to identify his cause. Against an opponent he says in the *First Defence:* "Then you inveigh against the common people as being blind and brutish, ignorant of the art of governing; you say there's nothing more empty, more vain, more inconstant, more uncertain than they. All which is very true for yourself, and it's true likewise of the rabble, but not of the middle sort, amongst whom the more prudent men, and most skillful in affairs generally are found."

BIBLIOGRAPHY

Clark, D. L. *John Milton at St. Paul's School, a Study of Ancient Rhetoric in English Renaissance Education.* New York, 1948.

Fletcher, Harris. *Contributions to a Milton Bibliography.* Urbana, 1931.

Jebb, Sir Richard. *Samson Agonistes and the Hellenic Drama.* Proceedings of the British Academy. London, 1908.

Langdon, Ida. *Milton's Theory of Poetry and Fine Art.* New Haven, 1924.

Milton, John. *Complete Poems and Major Prose*; ed. by M. Y. Hughes. New York, 1957.

————. *Samson Agonistes*; ed. by A. W. Verity. Cambridge, 1912.

————. *The Works of.* 18 vols. New York, 1931–1938.

Muir, Kenneth. *John Milton.* London, 1955.

Stevens, D. H. *Reference Guide to Milton from 1800 to the Present Day.* Chicago, 1930.

Thompson, Elbert N. S. *John Milton. A Topical Bibliography.* New Haven, 1916.

9 · William Davenant (1606–1668) and
Thomas Hobbes (1588–1679)

OF THE COMMONWEALTH MEN, Milton alone wrote important literary criticism. During this period the only other substantial criticism by Englishmen was written in Paris by two royalist exiles, Sir William Davenant and Thomas Hobbes. Davenant prefaces his heroic poem *Gondibert* (and a poor poem it is, too) with a letter to Hobbes, and Hobbes answers his letter. These letters reveal how much the English exiles were influenced by French criticism and show the kind of criticism that is going to be brought back to England with Charles II. They are of great interest for two reasons. First, they are, as might be expected, completely without the middle-class note that sounds in Milton's remarks. Second, they help mark the transition from Renaissance to neoclassical criticism in English thought.

Something had gone out of life. With all their rule-making the Renaissance critics never forgot that the poet is divine, that he is inspired. In Davenant and Hobbes the fire is gone. Inspiration is replaced by reason, imagination by fancy. As you read them you realize that they believe that all the poet needs to do to write a great poem is to follow the rules. Since both are convinced of the worth of *Gondibert*, you suspect that neither would recognize great poetry if he saw it.

Davenant begins his letter by praising the ancient epic poets. When he considers the moderns, however, he can find only two writers of heroic poems who are worthy of notice: Tasso and Spenser. But Tasso is criticized for his fables and Spenser

56

for his obsolete language and his allegories ("resembling a continuance of extraordinary Dreams; such as excellent Poets, and Painters, by being over studious, may have in the beginning of Feavers"). Davenant then explains why he has set his poem in Christian times. Then he tells why he has chosen Italy instead of England as the scene of his poem. Living in France in an age when the ideal of literature was becoming more and more universal and cosmopolitan, he has none of the vigorous national feeling of Spenser. Next he tells us that he has taken the patterns of manners from courts and camps. Finally he defends (in a manner that looks forward to the "Heroic Plays" of the Restoration) his choice of love versus honor as his subject matter.

In Hobbes' reply to Davenant's letter we discover the philosophical basis for the neoclassical attitude. For Hobbes all is simple, all is clear. The universe is divided into three regions: celestial, aerial, and terrestrial; the world into three: court, city and country. Hence, there are three divisions of poetry: heroic, scommatic [satiric], and pastoral. A further distinction is made in the manner of representation: narrative or dramatic. There are, therefore, only six kinds of poetry possible: epic, tragedy, satire, comedy, pastoral, and pastoral comedy. They err, says Hobbes, who take for poetry all that is written in verse. Sonnets, epigrams, and eclogues are not poetry. The subject of a poem is the "manners of men."

Hobbes now gives the basic assumptions behind his criticism. He writes that he can see no reason why a poet should want to be thought to speak by inspiration since inspiration is but another word for madness. "Time and Education begets experience, Experience begets memory; Memory begets Judgment and Fancy; Judgment begets the strength and structure; and Fancy begets the ornaments of a Poem."

This passage expresses a sort of intellectual and spiritual equalitarianism to which the concept of genius is foreign. A man who has lived as long and has had as much experience as another has equal memory from which the main qualifications necessary for the poet are derived. The strength and structure of the poem are primary. Fancy merely supplies the ornaments.

Fancy is a weak word, and it is meant to be. Inspiration and imagination are pushed out of the picture. Fancy itself is bound to "true philosophy," and the making of a poem by the "workmanship of Fancy" is exactly like making a new scientific instrument. When the Romantics later claim that the essence of the poet and poetry is left out of neoclassical criticism, they are thinking of criticism such as this.

No doubt, too, the down-to-earth approach of Davenant and Hobbes can be considered in part as a reaction against the strained images of the so-called metaphysical poets who flourished in the first half of the seventeenth century. Davenant scorns those who admire "what are commonly called *Conceits*, things that sound like the knacks or toys of ordinary *Epigramatists*." Hobbes hits at the same poets when he demands that expression be clear and that the poet eschew using words that are hard to understand. He declaims against "the ambitious obscurity of expressing more than is perfectly conceived; or perfect conception in fewer words than it requires. Which expressions, though they have had the honor to be called strong lines, are indeed no better than Riddles, and not only to the Reader, but also (after a little time) to the Writer himself dark and troublesome." He is equally against needlessly difficult stanzas and rhyme schemes. Anything that stands in the way of clear expression is bad.

Davenant's view of the political function of the poet is, as might be expected of a royalist exile, exactly opposite to Milton's. Poetry helps keep the commonality satisfied with their prince. "Princes and nobles being reformed and made Angelical by the Heroics," he writes, "will be predominant lights, which the people cannot choose but use for direction; as glow worms take in, and keep the Sun's beams till they shine, and make day themselves."

He defends the stage in a remarkable way against the Puritans who closed the theater. He says that any government lacks wisdom which attempts to keep the people serious and grave and to make every subject a statesman. No such government, he implies, will long endure. The people must be given the diversions of pleasure and mirth.

When Charles II came back to England this was his policy.

In order to rule more easily he allowed the people the diversions the Commonwealth had denied them.

BIBLIOGRAPHY

Dowlin, C. M. *Sir William Davenant's Gondibert, its Preface, and Hobbes' Answer.* Philadelphia, 1934.

Harbage, Alfred. *Sir William D'Avenant, Poet Venturer, 1606–1668.* Philadelphia, 1935.

Nethercot, A. H. *Sir William D'Avenant, Poet Laureate and Playwright-Manager.* Chicago, 1938.

Spingarn, J. E., ed. *Critical Essays of the Seventeenth Century.* 5 vols. Oxford, 1908–1909.

Thorpe, C. D. *The Aesthetic Theory of Thomas Hobbes, with Special Reference to His Contribution to the Psychological Approach in English Literary Criticism.* Ann Arbor, 1940.

10 · Boileau (1636–1711)

THE *Art of Poetry*, published in France in 1674 by Boileau, remains one of the most famous works of criticism ever written. As long as the neoclassical doctrines ruled the world of letters, Boileau's name was supreme. Afterward he became the main target of the Romantic critics. Yet, Boileau owes his eminence neither to genius nor profundity but to the circumstance that the virtues and limitations of his mind were exactly those of his age.

At the time he wrote, a period of individualism—which had degenerated into excess and bad taste—had passed away and a new and better-ordered period of literature had arrived. He has at times been given credit for single-handedly turning the tide of taste. He did nothing of the sort. Neoclassicism was well established in France before he wrote his verse essay. What he did, and this should be sufficient claim to fame, was to express the new attitude better than anyone before him and so well that there was no need to do it again.

He was anything but original. The greater part of his *Art of Poetry* is familiar to us from Horace and the Renaissance critics, but he restates these critics in the terms of that *common sense* which was rapidly becoming the ideal of the nation. He begins his treatise with a bow to the notion that the writer must first of all have genius—a notion whose implications he pushes aside since genius cannot be taught. He wants to teach the poet to write according to the rules of reason, as can be easily seen by italicizing the key words of the following passage:

Whate'er you write of pleasant or sublime,
Always let *sense* accompany your rime;
Falsely they seem each other to oppose,—
Rime must be made with *reason's* laws to close;
And when to conquer her you bend your force,
The mind will triumph in the noble course;
To *reason's* yoke she quickly will incline,
Which, far from hurting, renders her divine;
But if neglected, will easily stray,
And master *reason*, which she should obey.
Love *reason* then, and let whate'er you write
Borrow from her its beauty, force and light.

Authors ought to "fly excess" and aim at sense. Truth and beauty are one. The poet uses his reason to discover truth in nature. Why do the Greek and Roman writers still live? Because of the truth of their observations. And so, if you want to learn how a father acts toward his son, open your Terence. It is plain that what Boileau means by nature is human nature and that he believes that this is best portrayed in the classics. The advice to study nature ends up by being the advice to study the classics.

Manners, even in the narrowest sense, are becoming all important, as they usually do in a settled society. The old Renaissance search for all knowledge is now under suspicion, since it may lead to pedantry. The ideal of the age is the *honnête homme*, the reasonable gentleman who will express himself well in the commonplaces of the day but will not bore others with his own special learning. Men wear wigs; their poetry also should be politely bewigged. The unsure man going into society wants not so much to make an impression as to avoid blunders. So Boileau is not so much trying to make a poet as to keep a poet from making a fool of himself. This the rules will help him do.

Boileau not only tells what ancient poets it is best to imitate, but gives rules for pastoral, elegy, sonnet, epigram, ode, satire, and drama. All the accepted genres are here. Nor does Boileau hesitate to tell the poet how to write each line. He gives the rules for the caesura and the hiatus, tells when to use words that end with a vowel and when not to. All of these precepts are meant to make the verse clear and the communication easy.

No doubt many of his suggestions do have practical value for French verse if they are not hardened into ineluctable rules. But they are. Furthermore, many of his rules do not even have this in their favor. He tells us he follows reason, but why a given rule is reasonable he does not say. For instance, if you write for the theater, you must keep the three unities. A Spanish poet may put the whole life of a man in one play,

> But we, that are to reason's rule confined,
> Will that with art the poem be designed,
> That unity of action, time, and place
> Keep the stage full and all our labors grace.

No one, he declares, will fail to keep the unities of action, time, and space when writing for a French audience. If he does fail to, the audience will walk out on him.

The rules Boileau gives remind us of the precepts of the Renaissance critics. There is, however, a difference, and it is an important one. The Renaissance critics said do thus and so because it was done by the ancients; Boileau says do thus and so because common sense and reason demand it. The "follow the ancients" of the Renaissance allows the poet a degree of freedom which is absent from Boileau's "follow the ancients because they, too, follow the rules of common sense." A Renaissance poet like Ronsard, who could soar in his poetry by imitating the Greeks Pindar and Anacreon, is considered excessive by Boileau and is placed below the more correct Malherbe. It is really too dangerous to attempt to be a Ronsard. Write clearly and naturally; if you attempt more you are likely to be obscure.

> More pleased we are to see a river lead
> His gentle streams along a flowery mead,
> Than from high banks to hear loud torrents roar,
> With foamy waters, on a muddy shore.
> Gently make haste, of labor not afraid;
> A hundred times consider what you've said;
> Polish, repolish, every color lay,
> And sometimes add, but oftener take away.

This is the taste of the age. The fountains of Versailles are preferred to the peaks and chasms of the Alps. Nature, yes, but nature that is subordinate to man as he lives in the city and the court.

The poet must always keep *la bienséance,* decorum. This means not only using descriptions appropriate to the age and position of the person being described, but it means avoiding all that is "low." Give your characters those happy Roman names that seem made for poetry: Hector, Alexander, Ulysses, and Achilles. Only the ignorant poet will choose a barbarous, medieval name like Childebrand. The poet's diction must be poetic, not common. Only a trivial fool would describe in a poem about the flight of the Hebrews from Egypt,

> . . . a child who "with his little hand
> Picked up the shining pebbles from the sand."

Why? we might naïvely ask. Boileau answers:

> Such objects are too mean to stay our sight;
> Allow your work a just and noble flight.

Poetry teaches, and vulgar things should not be taught. In the Renaissance, Vida could write:

> When things are small the terms should still be so
> For low words please us when the theme is low.

But Boileau, with his uneasy gentility, is afraid of the "low" even in those places where previous critics would allow it. So he contradicts Vida with this verse:

> In all you write be neither low nor vile:
> The meanest theme may have a proper style.

So it was that, when Shakespeare was introduced into France in the next century, followers of Boileau objected to *Hamlet* because Hamlet uses the low word "rat," and to *Othello* because of the word "handkerchief."

Where the Renaissance critics disagree, Boileau joins forces with the conservatives. Tasso and Guarini could demand the right to use Christian subjects, but not Boileau. He allows only classical gods and goddesses. Christian machinery (like that in Milton's *Paradise Lost*) will not please:

> Besides, what pleasure can it be to hear
> The howlings of repining Lucifer,
> Whose rage at your imagined hero flies,
> And oft with God himself disputes the prize.

Obviously, a poet cannot live on what the booksellers pay him for his poems. But in happy and well-ordered France the correct poet is, as was Boileau, favored by noble patrons and the grand monarch himself. For here

> . . . verse is cherished by the great,
> And now none famish who deserve to eat.
> What can we fear when virtue, arts, and sense,
> Receive the stars' propitious influence,
> When a sharp-sighted prince, by early grants,
> Rewards your merit, and prevents your wants?
> Sing then his glory, celebrate his fame;
> Your noblest theme is his immortal name.

BIBLIOGRAPHY

Albalat, Antoine. *L'Art poétique de Boileau*. Paris, 1929.

Bonfanti, Mario. *L'Art poétique di Boileau e i suoi problemi*. Naples, 1957.

Brody, Jules. *Boileau and Longinus*. Genève, 1958.

Clark, A. F. B. *Boileau and the French Classical Critics in England (1660–1830)*. Paris, 1925.

Haley, Marie Philip. *Racine and the Art poétique of Boileau*. Baltimore, 1938.

Magne, Emile. *Bibliographie générale des œuvres de Nicolas Boileau-Despréaux*. Paris, 1929.

11 · Dryden (1631–1700)

DRYDEN IS Boileau's contemporary. He belongs to the same clan. Writing after the Restoration of the Stuarts, he is one of the group who helped form the neoclassical school of literature in England. Yet between him and Boileau there is an unbridgeable chasm. Dryden, a good English poet, has behind him the tradition of the great poetry of the age of Shakespeare.

His major critical work, *An Essay of Dramatic Poesy* (1668, revised in 1684) is in the form of a dialogue. The speakers are Neander (Dryden himself), Crites (Sir Robert Howard), Lisideius (Sir Charles Sedley), and Eugenius (Lord Buckhurst). By using the dialogue form Dryden is able to present the various critical points of view that agitated literary circles at this time. Rather than giving a series of dogmatic statements, as might Boileau, he has Eugenius contend that the plays of the last age are better than ours, Crites, uphold the ancient drama, Lisideius argue that the French playwrights are better than the English, and Neander defend the English.

Strangely enough, Dryden has been criticized for this very dialogue form which makes his essay such refreshing reading. Those detractors who have called Dryden a timeserver who shifted his politics as different rulers came to power say also his *Essay* is deliberately inconclusive so as to offend no one.

This is not so. Dryden is attempting to help introduce into England the new standards of taste without denying those parts of the English tradition that he feels are still valuable. His head is with the French critics, but his heart beats in time to the great English poetry of the past. Rather than being an example of time serving, his *Essay* does for his age an almost unbelievably good job.

In the dialogue the "rules" are given a clear exposition by Crites. The unity of time, limiting the action of the play to twenty-four hours, is said to be the "nearest imitation of nature." The unity of place—one scene—is said to be natural, since it is difficult for the audience to consider one place, the stage, as many places. The unity of action is defended on the grounds that two actions would make not one play but two.

Eugenius takes the side of the moderns in the battle of the ancients versus the moderns. He accuses the ancients of having left love, "the most frequent of the passions," untouched. He contends that because science has progressed since the time of Aristotle, it follows that modern poetry may arrive at greater perfection—an interesting example of the neoclassical tendency to equate poetry with natural laws.

Lisideius claims that the best modern poets are the French. "We have been so long together bad Englishmen that we had not leisure to be good poets." Thanks to the great Cardinal Richelieu's protection of literature, France has produced a theater that surpasses not only that of England but of all Europe. The French have kept the rules. They have no absurd tragicomedies as do the English, and they have the good sense, unlike the English, not to represent death on the stage. Finally they have beautified drama by using rhyme, not blank verse.

Now Neander begins to speak. He argues that the rules of French poetry "will raise perfection higher where it is, but are not sufficient to give it where it is not." Nor can he admit the objections to tragicomedy. Comic relief can make the tragic even more tragic. Indeed English tragicomedy is "a more pleasant way of writing for the stage than was ever known to the ancients or moderns of any nation." English variety gives more pleasure to the audience than French unity. As for death and combats on the stage, "why may not our imagination as well suffer itself to be deluded with the probability of it as with any other thing in the play?"

Neander having defended the variety of English drama now turns to individual playwrights. Here Dryden's critical genius burns brightest. He gives a sound critical appreciation of the playwrights of the previous age.

To begin, then, with Shakespeare. He was the man who of all modern and perhaps ancient poets had the largest and most comprehensive soul. All the images of nature were still present to him, and he drew them not laboriously but luckily; when he describes anything, you more than see it, you feel it too. Those who accuse him to have wanted learning give him the greater commendation; he was naturally learned; he needed not the spectacles of books to read nature; he looked inwards and found her there. I cannot say he is everywhere alike; were he so, I should do him injury to compare him with the greatest of mankind. He is many times flat, insipid; his comic wit degenerating into clenches [puns], his serious swelling into bombast. But he is always great when some great occasion is presented to him; no man can say he ever had a fit subject for his wit and did not then raise himself as high above the rest of poets. . . . "As high as the cypresses that tower above the bending viburnums."

Good as this is, it is still the appreciation of one who believes in the rules. The implication here is that Shakespeare didn't need this type of learning, but everyone who is not Shakespeare does. His comment on Beaumont and Fletcher is less strikingly central. In speaking of them, however, he makes the interesting statement that in their plays the English vocabulary reached its perfection. The words added since then are superfluous.

His "character" of Jonson is good. He considers that Jonson is the most learned and judicious writer who ever wrote for the stage. He knew his own strength and managed it to advantage. He seldom put love scenes in his plays, since he knew his genius was not fitted for them. "Humor was his proper sphere; and in that he was delighted most to represent mechanical people." He borrowed boldly from the ancients, but "what would be theft in other poets is only victory in him."

Finally, Dryden compares the two great dramatists. "If I would compare him with Shakespeare, I must acknowledge him the more correct poet but Shakespeare the greater wit. Shakespeare was the Homer or father of our dramatic poets; Jonson was the Virgil, the pattern of elaborate writing; I admire him, but I love Shakespeare."

This is both admirable and honest. Shakespeare will not fit into the rules as well as Jonson, but Dryden loves him. Jonson he can only admire. And yet when Dryden picks a play to analyze it is not one of Shakespeare's but one of Jonson's that he chooses. He takes the *Silent Woman* and shows that according to the best rules of construction it is superior to the plays of the French. He could not do this as easily with one of Shakespeare's. The only real way he knows to talk about literature is the way Boileau and the other neoclassicists talk about it. And so, though his heart is with Shakespeare, he cannot give the *reasons* for Shakespeare's plays that he can for Jonson's. But at least he is honest enough not to let his set of critical principles blind him to greatness that cannot be measured by them.

So, though he remains a neoclassicist, he is a liberal one. There are even hints in his criticism of the national and historical approaches that the nineteenth century is going to bring forth. He suggests several times that what is good for the French is not necessarily good for the English. In this passage in which he explains that Shakespeare and Fletcher were as good in their age as Sophocles and Euripides in theirs, he approaches the historical view of poetry:

And one reason for that success is, in my opinion, this, that Shakespeare and Fletcher have written to the genius of the age and nation in which they lived; for though nature . . . is the same in all places, and reason too the same, yet the climate, the age, the disposition of the people, to which a poet writes, may be so different, that what pleased the Greeks would not satisfy an English audience.

Yet we would be guilty of the same lack of historical feeling for which we accuse the neoclassicists if we overemphasized insights such as this. That Dryden has them sets him apart, to be sure, but he probably felt more comfortable when he was giving the usual arguments in favor of rhyme in tragedy. He argues that in spite of the fact that Shakespeare, Jonson, and Fletcher have written their plays in blank verse, rhyme is better. The gentlemen in the audience are favorable to verse. Rhyme exalts the language above the level of common converse. "Tragedy, we know, is wont to image to us the minds and fortunes of noble persons, and to portray these exactly; heroic rhyme is

nearest nature, as being the noblest kind of modern verse."
This is the jargon of the age, and Dryden is of the age. The
main thing is not to make mistakes. "Verse . . . is a rule and
line by which [the poet] keeps his building compact and even,
which otherwise lawless imagination would raise either irregu-
larly or loosely. At least, if the poet commits errors with this
help, he would make greater and more without it; 'tis, in short,
a slow and painful, but surest kind of working."

BIBLIOGRAPHY

Bredvold, L. I. *The Intellectual Milieu of John Dryden.* Ann
    Arbor, 1934.
Dryden, John. *The Essays of;* ed. by W. P. Ker. 2 vols. Oxford,
    1926.
————. *Essay of Dramatic Poesy;* ed. by Thomas Arnold, re-
    vised by W. T. Arnold. Oxford, 1903.
————. *Essays on the Drama;* ed. by William Strunk. New
    York, 1898.
Huntley, F. L. *On Dryden's 'Essay of Dramatic Poesy.'* Ann
    Arbor, 1951.
Smith, D. N. *John Dryden.* Cambridge, 1950.

12 · Pope (1688–1744)

BY THE TIME Pope published his *Essay on Criticism* in 1711, the neoclassical movement had become firmly established in England. The great figure of Shakespeare had for the moment receded into the past, and Pope could allow himself to be much more rigorously French and neoclassical than Dryden's feeling for the poetry of the previous age had allowed him to be.

In Pope we are again in Boileau's well-ordered world. His very title, *Essay on Criticism*, restricts his remarks to critics and critical principles. He does not, as Dryden did, have to examine the actual literature that had been and was being written.

He starts out with the statement that good taste is as necessary to the critic as genius is to the poet, but that both demand to be restrained:

> Nature to all things fixed the limits fit.
> And wisely curbed proud man's pretending wit.

Nature is not what the Romantics are going to consider it. She is the standard, the rule, the bridle that curbs:

> First follow Nature, and your judgment frame
> By her just standard, which is still the same:
> Unerring nature! still divinely bright
> One clear, unchanged and universal light.
> Life, force and beauty, must to all impart,
> At once the source and end, and test of art.

The rules of poetry are to Pope, as to Boileau, natural and reasonable. Excess and enthusiasm in poetry must be restrained by the rules.

> Those rules of old discovered not divised,
> Are nature still, but nature methodized;
> Nature, like liberty, is but restrained
> By the same laws which first herself ordained.

The poet and critic must be constant readers of the ancients, because the ancients were the ones who discovered the rules of nature. When, says Pope, young Vergil thought of writing an epic, he, like young poets, scorned to follow any laws but nature's, "But when t'examine every part he came, Nature and Homer were, he found, the same."

This is the point. You do not have to look at nature. All you need to do is look at the ancients. For, says Pope, "To copy nature is to copy them."

Criticism and poetry are like physics. There are natural laws that govern both. Since those for poetry have already been discovered by the great classical writers, the critics' and poets' jobs have already been partly done. All they have to do is apply them in specific instances. This is essentially what good taste means.

Though he admits that the great ancients sometimes transgressed the rules, Pope warns moderns not to do so. If they do, they should at least have an ancient precedent to plead. Though he advises us to judge each work in the "spirit that its author writ," the only spirit which really satisfies him is the neoclassical one. He is against the conceits of the metaphysicals. The only really acceptable poetry is the poetry of common sense that he himself writes.

> True wit is nature to advantage dressed;
> What oft was thought, but ne'er so well expressed.

And it must be admitted that Pope does well by his own standards. The commonplaces of his criticism are given memorable statement in his couplets.

> In words, as fashions, the same rule will hold;
> Alike fantastic, if too new, or old:
> Be not the first by whom the new are tried
> Not yet the last to lay the old aside.

Or again:

> Avoid extremes, and shun the fault of such
> Who still are pleased too little or too much.

The great trouble with all of these admirably stated common-places is that they are so general as to be almost meaningless. Pope's *Essay* is like the schoolboy's theme, largely topic sentences with few concrete examples.

Pope wants the critic as well as the poet to be polite and polished. The *sprezzatura*, the effortless grace, of the Renaissance aristocrat is here, but is now called diffidence:

> Be silent when you doubt your sense
> And speak, though sure, with seeming diffidence.

And,

> Without good breeding truth is disapproved
> That only makes superior sense beloved.

The Renaissance love of learning is by this time tempered by the fear of pedantry. Pope is scornful of the "bookful blockhead." What he wants is the *honnête homme* of whom he gives a neat definition: "Though learned, well-bred; and though well-bred, sincere."

The last section of the *Essay*, which is devoted to the history of literary criticism, best reveals Pope's views. A believer in absolutes and rules, he has little or no sense of history.

Greek poetry was free but barbarous until Aristotle gave it laws. Horace is still as valuable for us as for his fellow Romans. He "talks us into sense." Then Pope gives a word or two to Dionysius, Petronius, and Quintilian. He appreciates, he tells us the "poet's fire" of Longinus, though little in his own criticism reflects it. The classical age was the golden one of criticism. License was suppressed by the laws of just critics and "Learning and Rome alike in empire grew."

Then the Dark Ages came. What the Goths left untouched the monks finished off. In such a light even a Roman Catholic like Pope looked upon the Middle Ages in the second decade of the eighteen century.

With the Renaissance, the ancient laws of literature were happily reestablished, spreading outward from Italy.

> But critic learning flourished most in France;
> The rules a nation, born to serve, obeys;
> And Boileau still in right of Horace sways.

> But we, brave Britons, foreign laws despised.
> And kept unconquered and uncivilized.

For Pope, Boileau is the culminating point of modern criticism, the true heir of Aristotle and Horace. England, alas, has been distressingly backward until the present age. But fortunately "wit's fundamental laws" have been restored in England by the "sounder few" who "durst assert the juster ancient cause." Now all is well. No further change is necessary. Like happy France, England has its own Boileau in Pope.

BIBLIOGRAPHY

Atkins, J. W. H. *English Literary Criticism: 17th and 18th Centuries*. London, 1951.

Dennis, John. *The Age of Pope*. London, 1928.

Durham, W. H., ed. *Critical Essays of the Eighteenth Century*. New Haven, 1915.

Elwin, W., and W. J. Courthope. *The Works of Alexander Pope*. 10 vols. London, 1871–1898.

Pope and his Contemporaries: Essays Presented to George Sherburn. Oxford, 1949.

Root, R. K. *The Poetical Career of Alexander Pope*. Princeton, 1938.

Sherburn, George. *The Early Career of Alexander Pope*. Oxford, 1934.

Sitwell, Edith. *Alexander Pope*. London, 1930.

Spence, Joseph. *Anecdotes, Observations and Characters of Books and Men*. London, 1820.

Stephen, Sir Leslie. *Alexander Pope*. London, 1880.

Tillotson, Geoffrey. *On the Poetry of Pope*. Oxford, 1938.

Warton, Joseph. *An Essay on the Genius and Writings of Pope*. 2 vols. London, 1756, 1782.

13 · Samuel Johnson (1709–1784)

ENGLISH neoclassical criticism has Dryden at the beginning, Pope in the middle, and Samuel Johnson at the end. Of the three, Pope is the strictest. Dryden at the beginning and Johnson at the end of the period are subject to influences which make the dogmatism of Pope's *Essay on Criticism* less easy for them to embrace.

Yet Johnson can be as dogmatic as anyone when he wants to be. Tory that he was, he had little or no sympathy for the new tastes in art, architecture, and literature that seemed to him to go along with Whiggism in politics. The essays in his periodical *The Rambler* (1749–1752) show a tendency to demand a neoclassical strictness in English verse that reminds one of Boileau. He can find no excuse for the English poets who are again imitating Spenser. For him the lovely Spenserian stanza is "at once difficult and unpleasing; tiresome to the ear from its uniformity, and to the attention by its length."

In his novel *Rasselas* (1759), true to his pedagogical ideal, Johnson has in the tenth chapter a dissertation upon poetry which gives in a clear and memorable form the basic neoclassical theory. In it we are told that the "province of poetry is to describe nature and passion, which are always the same." The poet must be learned. "To a poet nothing can be useless." But this does not mean that he delights in the strange or the different.

The business of a poet is to examine, not the individual, but the species; to remark general properties and large appearances. He does

74

not number the streaks of the tulip, or describe the different shades
of the verdure of the forest; he is to exhibit in his portraits of nature
such prominent and striking features, as recall the original to every
mind; and must neglect the minuter discriminations, which one may
have remarked, and another have neglected, for those characteristics
which are alike obvious to vigilance and carelessness.

No better statement of the neoclassical view of nature can
be found. Later, Romantic poets are deliberately going to set
about "numbering the streaks of the tulips."

But, Johnson continues, this general knowledge of nature is
only half of the poet's task. He then adds the essentials, as he
and like critics saw them. The poet must also learn the manners
of men in all walks of life. "He must divert himself of the prejudices of his age and country; he must consider right and wrong
in their abstracted and invariable states; he must disregard present laws and opinions, and rise to general and transcendental
truths, which will always be the same."

With such principles Johnson became an excellent practical
critic for those poets who were of his own school. His *Lives of
the Poets* could not be bettered in the sections where he deals
with Dryden and Pope, whose poetry is exactly what Johnson
thinks poetry should be ("If Pope be not a poet, where is poetry
to be found?"). But, as might be expected, Johnson is less
happy in writing about poets whose view of poetry is different.
Gray was feeling his way toward Romanticism and not only
avoided Johnson's favored heroic couplet, but chose subjects
from the Welsh, the Norse, and the early English "barbaric"
ages. Further, Gray had democratic leanings. Johnson cannot
overcome his prejudices. His critical judgments of Gray's poetry
are marred by an obvious desire to find as much wrong as
possible.

Even less to modern taste is Johnson's estimate of Milton.
Milton was a member of the regicide government and a Puritan;
Johnson a monarchist and Anglican. This in itself might have
been enough. But add to it the fact that Johnson's taste could
not honestly comprehend Milton's verse, and you get judgments
that are so magnificently wrongheaded that one gasps for
breath. For instance, "Lycidas" is "harsh." On the sonnets—

some of which have never been equaled in English—Johnson writes, "Of the best it can only be said that they are not bad."

Yet Johnson can show an independence of judgment that reminds us of Dryden. What saved Dryden from being a Boileau, we remember, was Shakespeare, whose very existence could make even Pope at times forget his rules. So it is not surprising that it is in Johnson's Preface to his *Shakespeare* (1765) that we find his most liberal critical utterances, though admittedly they exist side by side with some of his narrowest criticism.

He asks why Shakespeare has kept the favor of his countrymen and answers his question by declaring that it is because he avoided the "irregular combinations of fanciful invention," for "just representations of general nature. . . . In the writings of other poets a character is too often an individual; in those of Shakespeare it is commonly a species." In other words, Johnson sees a Shakespeare who followed Johnson's dictum and did not number the streaks of the tulip. Then, showing how taste has shifted since Dryden, Johnson praises Shakespeare because he does not make love the central passion of most of his dramas. In Dryden's time, love vs. honor was considered *the* theme of serious plays.

Yet much in Shakespeare is not acceptable to Johnson. "The end of writing is to instruct; the end of poetry is to instruct by pleasing," and Shakespeare is not moral enough. "He sacrifices virtue to convenience, and is so much more careful to please than to instruct that he seems to write without any moral purpose." For "he makes no just distribution of good or evil nor is he always careful to show in the virtuous a disapprobation of the wicked."

Indeed, Shakespeare is often lacking in propriety or decorum, Johnson thinks. His jokes are often gross, he neglects the equality of words to things, and he spoils his characters' speeches with idle conceits and contemptible equivocations. "A quibble is the golden apple for which he will always turn aside from his career or stoop from his elevation. A quibble, poor and barren as it is, gave him such delight that he was content to purchase it by the sacrifice of reason, propriety, and truth. A quibble was to him the fatal Cleopatra for which he lost the world, and was content to lose it."

This essay of Johnson's, though founded solidly upon neo-classical taste, strikes a blow at the unities of time and place from which they never recovered. What makes his blow so telling is that he destroys the unities of the neoclassicists with that very tool of common sense with which they had presumably been constructed.

The stricter neoclassicists argued that verisimilitude demanded that the same stage which in one act is called Alexandria be not called Rome in the next. Johnson exploded this by reminding us that the stage is a stage. The audience never thinks it *is* Alexandria. So there is no difficulty if it is called Rome in the next act. "It is false that any representation is mistaken for reality; that any dramatic fable in its materiality was ever credible, or for a single moment was ever credited." So much for the whole doctrine of credibility.

Nor does the unity of time have a more reasonable basis.. "Time is, of all modes of existence, most obsequious to the imagination; a lapse of years is as easily conceived as a passage of hours. In contemplation we easily contract the time of real actions, and therefore willingly permit it to be contracted when we only see their imitation."

Thus by the use of a grain more of reason, two of the unities are blown up. The only unity Johnson will admit as necessary is the unity of action. The last of the neoclassicists has shaken the walls of his own citadel. The Romantics are ready to pour through the breaches.

Johnson is perfectly aware of the damage he has done. He says, "I am almost frightened at my own temerity." He wants to believe in the old rules and even suspects there are reasons for them he has not been able to discover. But apologetic or not, he is clear that where he stands is not where Boileau stood.

The result of my inquiries . . . is that the unities of time and place are not essential to a just drama; that, though they may sometimes conduce to pleasure, they are always to be sacrified to the nobler beauties of variety and instruction; and that a play written with nice observation of critical rules is to be contemplated as an elaborate curiosity, as the product of superfluous and ostentatious art, by which is shown rather what is possible than what is necessary.

BIBLIOGRAPHY

Bate, W. J. *From Classic to Romantic, Premises of Taste in Eighteenth-Century England*. Cambridge, 1946.
———. *The Achievement of Samuel Johnson*. New York, 1955.
Bosker, Aisso. *Literary Criticism in the Age of Johnson*. Revised edition, Groningen, 1953.
Clifford, J. L. *Johnsonian Studies, 1887–1950; a Survey and Bibliography*. Minneapolis, 1951.
Hagstrum, J. H. *Samuel Johnson's Literary Criticism*. Minneapolis, 1952.
Houston, P. H. *Doctor Johnson: a Study in Eighteenth-Century Humanism*. Cambridge, 1923.
Johnson, Samuel. *The Critical Opinions of Samuel Johnson*. Arranged and compiled by Joseph E. Brown. New York, 1961.
———. *Lives of the English Poets*; ed. by G. B. Hill, 3 vols. Oxford, 1905.
———. *Prefaces and Dedications*; ed. by A. T. Hazen. New Haven, 1937.
———. *Works*. 9 vols. Oxford, 1825.
Raleigh, Sir Walter. *Johnson on Shakespeare*. Oxford, 1908.
Roberts, S .C. *Doctor Johnson*. London, 1926.
Roscoe, E. S. *Aspects of Dr. Johnson*. New York, 1928.
Smith, D. N., ed. *Eighteenth-Century Essays on Shakespeare*. Glasgow, 1903.
———, ed. *Shakespeare in the Eighteenth Century*. Oxford, 1928.
Spittal, J. K., ed. *Contemporary Criticisms of Dr. Samuel Johnson*. London, 1923.
Watkins, W. B. C. *Johnson and English Poetry Before 1660*. Princeton, 1936.

14 · Wordsworth (1770–1850) and Coleridge (1772–1834)

WHAT JOHNSON had done, destructive as it was of certain time-hallowed neoclassical concepts, had yet been done from a neo-classical point of view. He was still speaking as a member of the republic of letters to other members, whether they had lived on one or the other side of the English Channel. But not Wordsworth. He writes after the French Revolution has shattered the old way of life. The Rights of Man have been proclaimed. So Wordsworth speaks in his preface to the *Lyrical Ballads* (1800) not to a civilization settled in its patterns, but to man. After the old hierarchies had been discredited, and before the socialists came along to claim that the workingman was still in chains, the representatives of the new age felt that man had been liberated, not a man who happened to be born to a certain class of society, but man himself.

No longer are kings and princes the noblest subject of poetry, nor is keeping decorum the special purpose of the poet. Explaining his own poems, Wordsworth declares:

The principal object, then, proposed in these poems was to choose incidents and situations from common life, and to relate or describe them, throughout, as far as was possible in a selection of language really used by men, and, at the same time, to throw over them a certain coloring of imagination, whereby ordinary things should be presented to the mind in an unusual aspect, and, further, and above all, to make these incidents and situations interesting by tracing in them, truly though not ostentatiously, the primary laws of our nature. . . .

79

The view of what language the poet should use has completely changed since Dante. Avoid rustic language, Dante says in the *De vulgari eloquentia*, attempting to give polish to the rough medieval tongue of Italy. Since that time language has been so refined and polished that "poetic diction" has replaced ordinary speech. Use the language of ordinary men, especially rustics, the preface of Wordsworth urges.

Wordsworth is not interested in the manners of those who live in the city and the court. He wants poetry to deal with the "essential passions of the heart." Man in nature is better than man in the city. In rural occupations the "passions of men are incorporated with the beautiful and permanent forms of nature," not "nature methodized" but the fields and farms of England. The language of the farmers has been taken as the best because such men communicate with the "best objects from which the best part of language is originally derived."

Poetic diction and the personification of abstract ideas—the hallmarks of neoclassical verse—are bad because they are artificial. "Good poetry is the spontaneous overflow of powerful feelings," not the utterance of commonplaces in metrical language. Indeed, "the language of a large portion of every good poem . . . must necessarily, except with the reference to the meter, in no respect differ from that of good prose."

"What is a poet?" asks Wordsworth. No longer is he the singer of the great, the teacher of polite etiquette. "He is a man speaking to men: a man, it is true, endowed with more lively sensibility, more enthusiasm and tenderness, who has a greater knowledge of human nature and a more comprehensive soul than are supposed to be common among mankind; a man pleased with his own passions and volitions, and who rejoices more than other men in the spirit of life that is in him; delighting to contemplate similar volitions and passions as manifested in the goings-on of the universe and habitually impelled to create them where he does not find them."

Much of what we feel is fundamental to the Romantic view of life and literature is in this definition of the poet. Poetry, being the spontaneous overflow of emotion, is no longer learned, no longer a matter of the rules. At first glance this seems less hard on the poet than the old neoclassical demands on him, and it is, in one sense. In another, however, it tends to remove the poet further from ordinary people than did the neoclassical rules. The only real demand on the poet by the neoclassical critics was that he follow the rules. Wordsworth demands more. The poet must have certain gifts that are not common among mankind. This idea is soon going to lead to that of the poet as genius and, eventually, critics will want the poet to be not merely a superior man speaking to men but a superior man speaking only to superior men. But this is in the future. The important thing now in Wordsworth is the emphasis on the individualism of the poet, that pleasure in "his own passions and volitions" which makes him greatly different from the social poet of other periods.

And what is the purpose of poetry? To teach, said Horace, Scaliger, and Boileau. No, says Wordsworth. The only restriction the poet writes under is the "necessity of giving immediate pleasure to a human being possessed of that information which may be expected from him, not as a lawyer, a physician, a mariner, an astronomer, or a natural philosopher, but as a man."

Wordsworth thus answers Plato's complaint in the *Ion* that the poet knows less about chariot-racing than a charioteer. The answer is an easy one to give once the assumption is made that the poet is not a teacher of facts.

Poetry for Wordsworth is not merely another social or intellectual activity. It is "the breath and finer spirit of all knowledge; it is the impassioned expression which is in the countenance of all science." The truth of science is remote. It is not made a part of our "natural and inalienable inheritance" until the poet uses it. A scientific invention is not a human object until the poet carries sensation into its midst. To give a recent example that Wordsworth would have liked, the airplane was long a useful and beneficial invention, but it remained a mere object of science until such writers as Antoine de Saint-Exupéry made it "palpably material to us as enjoying and suffering beings."

Poetry is no longer a matter of reason and of rules. Such a Renaissance figure as Scaliger could believe his poetry, his botany, his physics, and his grammatical and rhetorical studies to be all of a piece. Wordsworth cannot. For him poetry exists on a separate and special plane. It deals not with the products of the intellect but with those of the imagination, the feelings. "Poetry," he says in his famous definition, "is the spontaneous, overflow of powerful feelings: it takes its origin from emotion recollected in tranquillity: the emotion is contemplated till, by a species of reaction, the tranquillity gradually disappears, and an emotion, kindred to that which was before the subject of contemplation, is gradually produced, and does itself actually exist in the mind."

From what Wordsworth says of the birth and nature of poetry, this pattern seems to emerge. The poet looks at nature. His emotions are aroused. In tranquillity he recalls his emotions. These emotions are made into a poem with the help of images of those things in nature which aroused the poet's emotions in the first place. The reader looks at the poem. The images of nature in the poem—alight with the poet's emotions—arouse in the reader emotions similar to those the poet had in the first place. Is this not, in essence, the way Wordsworth views the relations of the poet to his reader? Communication takes place in the realm of the emotions not that of ideas, commonplace or otherwise.

The weakest portion of this stimulating preface comes when Wordsworth discusses meter. After saying that the greater portion of the language of every good poem· does not differ from prose, he is forced to ask himself why, then, he writes in meter instead of prose. His answer is not very satisfactory, mainly because he has, in his opposition to the older school, attacked every other exaltation of language as against the naturalism he believes in. So he begins by saying that meter puts bounds on the excitement of poetry that otherwise might be too powerful or too painful. This simply isn't true, as he should have realized, since he later points out, this time justly, that meter intensifies emotion. Actually, he has no reasoned answer to the question he asks himself, so he lamely says, "Why should I be condemned for attempting to superadd to such description the charms which, by the consent of all nations, is acknowledged to exist in metrical language?" That this breaker of critical idols should be forced to appeal to authority is evidence of his insecurity on this question. Surely his major concern in all other parts of the essay is that his readers reject authority. "One request," he writes, "I must make of my reader, which is that in judging of these poems he would decide by his own feelings genuinely, and not by reflection upon what will probably be the judgment of others." Wordsworth's putting feeling as almost the opposite of judgment can lead in its most extreme form to the often-heard remark, "I don't know anything about poetry (or music or art), but I know what I like."

His friend and collaborator Coleridge takes the trouble to examine and correct Wordsworth's views on language and meter. He does it seventeen years later in his *Biographia Literaria*. Coleridge acutely remarks that Wordsworth's own theory of language is based on a *selection* of the language of rustics. Now, Coleridge says, if you remove the provincial terms of speech from a peasant's language you no longer have rustic language at all. You have the language that any man speaks. Thus he denies Wordsworth's main assertion that a special virtue is in the speech of those in close communication with nature. Yet, though he will not accept Wordsworth's theory, he is in complete agreement with him as to the falseness and artificiality of much of the verse of the preceding generation. Writing later than Wordsworth, at a time when the Romantic movement has more partisans, he can be more reasonable and less polemical than Wordsworth.

So, on the question of meter, too, he can correct his colleague's extreme statements. He affirms not only that there is diction that is appropriate in metrical language and not in prose, but that there are phrases that are acceptable in prose that would not be in poetry. He then clinches his argument by examining Wordsworth's own verse and proving that Wordsworth did not follow his own theory. "Were there excluded from Mr. Wordsworth's poetic composition all that a literal adherence to the theory of his Preface would exclude, two thirds at least of the marked beauties of his poetry must be erased."

Coleridge's contributions to criticism go far beyond his corrections of Wordsworth's slips. In the realm of practical criticism his discussion of Shakespeare is one of the Alps of English criticism. He says, with truth, "I was the first in time who publicly demonstrated, to the full extent of the position, that the supposed irregularity and extravagances of Shakespeare were the mere dreams of a pedantry that arraigned the eagle because it had not the dimensions of a swan."

Coleridge will hardly deign to argue with the rules of the neo-classicists. His view of poetry is organic, not mechanical. Real poetry is the union of the heart and head and can never be measured by yardsticks. "A poem is that species of composition, which is opposed to works of science, by proposing for its immediate object pleasure, not truth; and from all other species (having this object in common with it), it is discriminated by proposing to itself such delight from the whole, as is compatible with a distinct gratification from each component part."

The poet is born, not made. Not the recipes of the arts of poetry but the shaping power of the poet's imagination is what gives poetry its distinction.

The poet, described in ideal perfection, brings the whole soul of man into activity, with the subordination of its faculties to each other according to their relative worth and dignity. He diffuses a tone and spirit of unity, that blends, and, as it were, fuses, each into each, by that synthetic and magical power, to which I would exclusively appropriate the name of imagination. This power, first put in action by the will and understanding, and retained under their irremissive, though gentle and unnoticed, control reveals itself in the balance or reconcilement of opposite or discordant qualities: of sameness with difference; of the general, with the concrete; and the idea, with the image; the individual, with the representative; the sense of novelty and freshness, with old and familiar objects; a more than usual state of emotion, with more than usual order, judgement ever awake and steady self-possession, with enthusiasm and feeling profound or vehement; and while it blends and harmonizes the natural and the artificial, still subordinates art to nature; the manner to the matter; and our admiration of the poet to our sympathy with the poetry.

BIBLIOGRAPHY

Banerjee, Srikumar. *Critical Theories and Poetic Practice in the 'Lyrical Ballads.'* London, 1931.
Barstow, M. L. *Wordsworth's Theory of Poetic Diction.* Yale University Press, 1917.

Beatty, Arthur. *William Wordsworth: His Doctrine and Art in Their Historical Relations.* Madison, 1922.

Beer, J. B. *Coleridge, the visionary.* London, 1959.

Coleridge, S. T. *Biographia Epistolaris;* ed. by Turnbull: 2 vols. London, 1911.

————. *Biographia Literaria, or Biographical Sketches of My Literary Life and Opinions;* ed. by J. A. Symons. New York, 1908.

————. *Lectures and Essays on Shakespeare and Some Other Old Poets and Dramatists.* London, 1907.

————. *The Friend.* 3rd ed. London, 1837.

————. *Letters of Coleridge;* ed. by E. H. Coleridge. 2 vols. London, 1895.

————. *Miscellanies, Aesthetic and Literary;* collected and edited by A. J. George. Boston, 1895.

Fogle, R. H. *The Idea of Coleridge's Criticism.* Berkeley and Los Angeles, 1962.

Garrod, H. W. *Wordsworth: Lectures and Essays.* Oxford, 1923.

Helmholtz, A. A. *The Indebtedness of Samuel Taylor Coleridge to August Wilhelm von Schlegel.* Madison, 1907.

Henley, E. F. *Wordsworthian Criticism, 1945–1949; an Annotated Bibliography.* New York, 1960.

Howard, Claud. *Coleridge's Idealism: A Study of Its Relationship to Kant and to the Cambridge Platonists.* Boston, 1924.

Huxley, Aldous. *Holy Face and Other Essays.* London, 1929.

Jones, H. J. F. *The Egotistical Sublime: a History of Wordsworth's Imagination.* London, 1954.

Kennedy, V. W. *Samuel Taylor Coleridge.* Baltimore, 1935.

Lucas. F. L. *The Decline and Fall of the Romantic Ideal.* New York, 1936.

McKenzie, Gordon. *Organic Unity in Coleridge.* Berkeley, 1939.

Muirhead, J. H. *Coleridge as Philosopher.* London, 1930.

Newton, Annabel. *Wordsworth in Early American Criticism, 1824–1860.* Chicago, 1928.

Raleigh, Sir Walter. *Wordsworth.* London, 1903.

Richards, I. A. *Coleridge on Imagination.* 2nd ed. New York, 1950.

Sherwood, Margaret. *Coleridge's Imaginative Conception of the Imagination.* Wellesley, 1937.

Smith, N. C., ed. *Wordsworth's Literary Criticism.* London, 1906.

Wordsworth, W. *Lyrical Ballads*; A *reprint*; ed. with introd. by H. Littledale. Oxford, 1911.

——. *Prose Works*; ed. by William Knight. 2 vols. London and New York, 1896.

15 · Victor Hugo (1802–1885)

WHETHER because neoclassicism lasted longer in France or was, and still is, as many French writers claim, more sympathetic to the Latin genius, the fact remains that the critical writing of the French Romantics not only was later in time but is more self-consciously polemical than that of the English. Though a good part of the Romantic criticism in all countries was in open reaction to the neoclassical school, much of French Romantic criticism seems more than that. It is pervaded by a desire to turn topsy-turvy the old rules, to arrive at new standards by deliberately standing the old ones on their heads.

Victor Hugo's preface to his drama *Cromwell*, published in 1827, is the best known and most spectacular of the treatises of the French school. His fundamental argument is that Romantic art is modern art. Times have changed and art must change along with them. He blows a trumpet to rally the young men to the standard of the present.

Hugo refuses to accept the doctrine that literature has nothing to do with society. He declares that the human race "was once a child; it was once a man; we are now looking on at its impressive old age. . . . Now as poetry is always superimposed upon society, we propose to try to demonstrate, from the form of its society, what the character of the poetry must have been in those three great ages of the world . . . primitive times, ancient times, modern times."

In primitive times man is so close to God that all of his dreams are visions. God, the soul, and creation are the threefold mystery he sings. He is a nomad. He is unrestrained. "Prayer

is his sole religion, the ode is his only form of poetry." Genesis
is the poem of primitive times.

In the second period, ancient times, the tribe becomes a nation. Migrations and voyages are characteristic of these times.
Poetry reflects the change and becomes epic. Homer is the great
poet. The history, too, of the ancients is epic. "Herodotus is a
Homer." That the epic is the dominant form is seen in the fact
that even the tragedy of the ancients is epic. The chorus is the
poet commenting on and completing his epic. The theater,
capable of holding thirty thousand spectators and vast spectacles, is epic by its very dimensions.

The ancient times pass away. A spiritual religion kills them
"and deposits in the corpse the germ of modern civilization."
With Christianity comes the new sentiment which is to make
the new period—melancholy. "Man, withdrawing within himself in the presence of these imposing vicissitudes, began to take
pity upon mankind, to reflect upon the bitter disillusionments
of life. Of this sentiment, which to Cato, the heathen, was de-
spair, Christianity fashioned melancholy."

Thus, like Guarini in the Italian Renaissance, Hugo sees that
the perfect imitation of the ancients which the classicizing
critics demanded is impossible because we are no longer pagans.
The transformation of the world that Christianity has wrought
has changed the soul of men. A person raised in the Christian
tradition could never, no matter how he tried, feel the same way
about life as a pagan Greek or Roman. When feelings change,
art must change too.

The early ages of Christianity were marked by great catas-
trophes, which were also great spectacles. "Melancholy and
meditation, the demons of analysis and controversy appear at
the same moment, and, as it were, hand in hand." Now the art
that springs from this period "will set about doing as nature
does, mingling in its creations—but without confounding them
—darkness and light, the grotesque and the sublime; in other
words, the body and the soul, the beast and the intellect." So
a new principle, a new type is introduced into poetry, the grotesque. The new art form is comedy. The grotesque, the ab-
normal, the horrible, now dominate: Dante in poetry, the gar-

goyles of the cathedrals in stone. Side by side with the grotesque
stands the sublime.

Three burlesque Homers stand upon the threshold of modern
poetry: Ariosto in Italy, Cervantes in Spain, Rabelais in France.
The grotesque is everywhere creatively allied with the beautiful
in a way that antiquity could not conceive. No ancient could
have written *Beauty and the Beast*.

For a long time the grotesque overshadowed the sublime. A
new genius established the true balance. He was Shakespeare.
He molded together "the grotesque and the sublime, the terrible
and the absurd, tragedy and comedy." He created the new,
culminating poetic form of modern times, the drama.

Only the drama is complete poetry. The earlier forms, the
ode and the epic, have poetry only in the germ. But the modern
era is dramatic, and being dramatic, lyric; for "it is lyric poetry
above all that befits the drama." Everything in modern poetry
leads to the drama.

Nothing could better represent the Romantics' desire to
smash neoclassicism than these theories of Hugo. The Middle
Ages, which the neoclassicists had scorned as "Gothick" and
barbarous, are acclaimed by Hugo as the seedbed of modern
literature. For the decorum and restraint beloved by Pope and
Boileau, Hugo substitutes the grotesque and the sublime. He is
as much for the extremes as they were for the golden mean.

Naturally, Hugo attacks the unities of time and space. He
scorns the rules. In their place he puts the rights of genius.
The poet now takes his place upon the stage as a hero, a Napoleon who can sweep all before him. "It would be strange, if in
this age, liberty, like the light, should penetrate everywhere except to the one place where freedom is most natural—the do-
main of thought. Let us take the hammer to theories and poetic
systems. Let us throw down the old plastering that conceals the
façade of art. There are neither rules nor models. . . ."

Though the poet uses nature, art and nature are distinct. The
drama is a concentrating mirror which intensifies, rather than
merely reflects, the light of nature. Everything that exists in history, in life, in man, can be in the drama. Particularly important
is its ability to give life to the past. For Hugo, the historical

drama is the most satisfactory of dramas since it performs this creative function. The verse for the new drama should be free, outspoken, sincere. The language should be modern. "The human intellect is always on the march." The French language of the seventeenth and eighteenth centuries cannot be the language of the nineteenth.

Everything is on the move. Progress is in the air. The new criticism will be founded, says Hugo, on "taste, the common sense of genius."

People generally will understand that writers should be judged, not according to rules and species, which are contrary to nature and art, but according to the immutable principles of the art of composition and the special laws of their individual temperaments.

BIBLIOGRAPHY

Berret, P. *Victor Hugo*. Paris, 1927.
Brunet, Georges. *Victor Hugo*. Paris, 1935.
Daudet, Léon. *Flambeaux*. Paris, 1929.
Grant, E. M. *The Career of Victor Hugo*. Cambridge, 1945.
Hugo, V. M. *La Préface de Cromwell*. Paris, 1897.
———. *Works of Victor Hugo*; tr. by G. B. Ives. New York, 1909.
Josephson, M. *Victor Hugo, a Realistic Biography of the Great Romantic*. New York, 1942.
Swinburne, A. *A Study of Victor Hugo*. London, 1886.

16·Goethe (1749–1832)

IT IS INTERESTING to compare the views on literature of Goethe, the greatest of German writers, with those of Hugo. Goethe lived so long and in such a rich period of his country's literary and cultural history that a full sketch of his criticism would demand a complete book. So much of it is imbedded in his poetry, novels, and plays and so little can be found in anything resembling a critical treatise that it is hard for the student to gain a clear conception of it.

Starting as a member of the wild and youthful *Sturm und Drang* (Storm and Stress) movement, he was responsible for much of the Romantic writing to which it gave birth, but he himself developed beyond it. He refused to remain in the posture of youthful defiance, and as he grew older he turned away from the extremes of even those Romantic poets who hailed him as their father.

His mature critical attitude is best seen in the *Conversations* his disciple Eckermann gave to the world. In these informal remarks we find that concern with culture in the broad rather than in the strictly literary sense that is central to his view of poetry. As a result one reads Goethe less as a theoretician of literature than for the ripe wisdom of one who deeply appreciates the problems of the poet.

Yet Goethe expresses himself on certain matters that are within the scope of this book. He looks upon poetry not as an individual matter but as "the universal possession of mankind, revealing itself everywhere, and at all times, in hundreds and hundreds of men. . . ." He adds that "the gift of poetry is by no means so very rare, and that nobody need think very much of himself because he has written a good poem." So true is this for Goethe that the question of plagiarism doesn't exist for him. When he and Schiller worked together, he tells us, neither attached the slightest importance as to who contributed what. "What matters the mine and thine?" He can write his poems in the rhythms of Shakespeare and Mozart without feeling that he is "stealing," and he is perfectly willing for others to use his own poetry in like manner.

Since poetry is a universal possession, the poetry of the future cannot be confined within national boundaries. The age of world literature is at hand. Yet, because of his preoccupation with Hellenism, Goethe will not look at world literature in a truly comparative way. "If," he says, "we really want a pattern, we must always return to the ancient Greeks, in whose works the beauty of mankind is constantly represented. All the rest we must look at only historically. . . ."

Goethe cannot accept the demands so often made by politicians that the poet use his art as an instrument of national policy. "If a poet would work politically, he must give himself up to a party; and as soon as he does that he is lost as a poet; he must bid farewell to his free spirit, his unbiased view, and draw over his ears the cap of bigotry and blind hatred." For, he says, "One can never make anything of a poet but what his nature intended him to be." Nothing, then, is more foolish than for critics and book reviewers to attempt to tell a writer how he should write. All they can do if they attempt it is to destroy him.

Although a product as well as an inspirer of the Romantic movement, the older Goethe detests extremes so much that he lumps all literature that goes under the name Romantic as sickly. "I call," he declares, "the classic *healthy*, the romantic *sickly*. In this sense the *Nibelungenlied* is as classic as the *Iliad*, for both are vigorous and healthy. Most modern productions are romantic, not because they are new, but because they are weak, morbid, and sickly; and the antique is classic, not because it is old, but because it is strong, fresh, joyous, and healthy. If men distinguish 'classic' and 'romantic' by those qualities, it will be easy to see our way clearly."

This so-called distinction can, of course, only make confusion worse confounded. The men of the early nineteenth century, Goethe himself included, taught the world to take the historical view of literature. By the time he uttered these words, it was possible to escape confusion by using "classic" and "romantic" as historical terms. His attempt to give the term "romantic" an entirely pejorative sense is unfortunate.

Yet, we can easily understand his motive. He is repelled by the excesses of the German "Romantic School." He sees the French Romanticists going to the same extreme that his own *Sturm und Drang* movement did earlier, and he is really thinking of such Frenchmen as Hugo when he says to Eckermann in 1830:

Extremes are never to be avoided in any revolution. In a political one, nothing is generally desired in the beginning but the abolition of abuses; but before people are aware, they are deep in bloodshed and horror. Thus the French in their present literary revolution desired nothing at first but a freer form; however, they will not stop there, but will reject the traditional contents together with the form. They begin to declare the representation of noble sentiments and deeds as tedious and attempt to treat of all sorts of abominations. Instead of the beautiful subjects from Grecian mythology, there are devils, witches and vampires; and the lofty heroes of antiquity must give place to jugglers and galley slaves. . . . A young man of talent, who would produce an effect and be acknowledged, and who is great enough to go his own way, must accommodate himself to the taste of the day—nay, must seek to outdo his predecessors in the horrible and frightful.

Yet Goethe sees, as we do today, that even the things he does not like in Romanticism are molding the literature of the future.

The extremes and excrescences which I have described will gradually disappear; but this great advantage will finally remain; besides a freer form, richer and more diversified subjects will have been attained, and no object of the broadest world and the most manifold life will be any longer excluded as unpoetical.

He was right. It was the Romantic movement which opened the way for the variety of later literature.

BIBLIOGRAPHY

Angelloz, J. F. *Goethe*; tr. from the French by R. H. Blackley. New York, 1958.

Atkins, S. P. *Goethe's Faust; a Literary Analysis.* Cambridge, 1958.

Bergsträsser, Arnold. *Goethe's Image of Men and Society.* Chicago, 1949.

Du Bos, Charles. *Goethe.* Paris, 1949.

Fauley, Barker. *A Study of Goethe.* Oxford, 1947.

Goethe, J. W. von. *Conversations of Goethe with Eckermann and Soret*; tr. by John Oxenford. London, 1892.

Hammer, Carl, ed. *Goethe after Two Centuries.* Baton Rouge, 1952.

Harnack, Otto. *Die klassische Asthetik der Deutschen. Würdigung der Kunst-Theoretischen Arbeiten Schiller's, Goethe's und ihrer freunde.* Leipzig, 1892.

International Goethe Bicentennial Convocation and Music Festival, Aspen, Colo., 1949. *Goethe and the Modern Age* . . .; ed. by Arnold Bergsträsser. Chicago, 1950.

Jantz, H. S. *Goethe's Faust as a Renaissance Man; Parallels and Prototypes.* Princeton, 1951.

Jessen, Mrs. Myra R. *Goethe als Kritiker der Lyrik; beiträge zu seiner ästhetik und seiner theorie.* . . . Bryn Mawr, 1932.

King, Rolf, ed. *Goethe on Human Creativeness and Other Goethe Essays.* Athens, 1950.

Lappmann, Wolfgang. *The German Image of Goethe.* Oxford, 1961.

Santayana, George. *Three Philosophical Poets: Lucretius, Dante and Goethe.* Cambridge, 1947.

Schweitzer, Albert. *Goethe: Five Studies*; tr. with an introd. by C. R. Joy. Boston, 1961.

Strich, Fritz. *Goethe and World Literature*; tr. by C. A. M. Sym. London, 1949.

Viëtor, Karl. *Goethe, the Thinker*; tr. by B. G. Morgan. Cambridge, 1950.

17 · Walt Whitman (1819–1892)

WHITMAN'S PREFACE to *Leaves of Grass* (1855) is the American equivalent of Hugo's preface to *Cromwell*. The same energy, the same sense of newness and freedom animate both. Yet, if anything, Whitman out-Hugo's Hugo. If the poet is a world-shaking genius to Hugo, he is a god, or better than a god, to Whitman.

Both Walt Whitman's poetry and his criticism are filled with his sense of uniqueness. He is an American and a democrat— a new species of bard. No one like him has existed before. As he looks across to the old countries he finds their writers, their best writers, tainted with ideas of caste and status. Shakespeare is against the common people, who are the life blood of democracy. His plays are "incarnated, uncompromising feudalism in literature." Scott's novels are "anti-democratic," and Tennyson's poems are full of "non-democracy."

He sees, though of course no one would suggest that this is the whole point, that politics and literature have been intertwined in the past and accepts—indeed, joyfully accepts—the fact that they will be in the future. He looks at the matter historically. The past was what the past had to be. Some of it is still clinging to opinions and manners in literature, but it will soon be dead. Now it is America's turn. America, "the stalwart and well-shaped heir who approaches." The future belongs to America and its literature. This literature shall be fittest for the new days as European literature was for the past.

"The Americans of all nations at any time upon the earth have the fullest poetical nature. The United States themselves are essentially the greatest poem. In the history of the earth hitherto the largest and most stirring appear tame and orderly to their ampler largeness and stir. Here at last is something in the doings of man that corresponds with the broadcast doings of the day and night. . . . Here are the roughs and beards and space and ruggedness and nonchalance that the soul loves." The United States of all nations, he says, has the best common people. All of their actions are unrhymed poetry. A gigantic and generous treatment of things will characterize the new poetry.

America is large. Its poetry will have this largeness. What is the need of imitation of the poets of Europe and the ancients? "As if the opening of the western continent by discovery and what has transpired since were less than the small theater of the antique or the aimless sleepwalking of the middle ages!"

The American poet will be as all-embracing as America itself. He incarnates its geography: the rivers, the mountains, the sea, the coasts, the trees, the birds. His subject matter will be the manners of men, yes, but of "young mechanics and of all free American workmen and workwomen." He will write about

the perfect equality of the female with the male . . . the large amativeness—the fluid movement of the population—the factories and mercantile life and laborsaving machinery—the Yankee swap —the New York fireman and the target excursion—the southern plantation life—the character of the northeast and of the northwest and southwest—slavery and the tremulous spreading of hands to protect it and the stern opposition to it which shall never cease till it ceases or the speaking of tongues and the moving of lips cease.

The American poet is worthy of his subject matter. "He is a seer . . . he is individual . . . he is complete in himself . . . the others are as good as he, only he sees it and they do not. He is not one of the chorus . . . he does not stop for any regulation . . . he is the president of regulation."

The new poet with his new and greater subject matter will not be bound by the old ideas of poetic diction or meter. The new rhythm of this poetry will be organic. "The fluency and ornaments of the finest poems or music or orations or recitations are not independent but dependent. All beauty comes from beautiful blood and a beautiful brain." American poetry will be as natural as the woods and rivers of America. Nothing which distorts honest shapes, particularly the human form, can be allowed. "Clean and vigorous children are jetted and conceived only in those communities where the models of natural forms are public every day." Here the connection between poetry and life is really put with a vengeance. It seems that the poor Europeans surrounded by baroque and rococo art will produce baroque and rococo children.

The American poet, dealing with American subject matters in new, American forms, is fortunate because he has a fit language in which to write. "It is the powerful language of resistance . . . it is the dialect of common sense. It is the speech of the proud and melancholy races and all who aspire. It is the chosen tongue to express growth faith self-esteem freedom justice equality friendliness amplitude prudence decision and courage." Seemingly its freedom will not even be restrained by commas!

All of these things, which will make the new poet and the new poetry, are born of freedom. No great poetry is possible without the idea of liberty. The poets are liberty's own voice. All other considerations are secondary to this grand idea. "The attitude of great poets is to cheer up slaves and horrify despots. The turn of their necks, the sound of their feet, the motions of their wrists, are full of hazard to the one and hope to the other."

Liberty, and not political liberty alone—though that is the causal factor—is what Whitman demands. "The old red blood and stainless gentility of great poets will be proved by their unconstraint." This negates at every point the old neoclassical doctrines, since if anything is characteristic of the neoclassicists it is restraint. For Whitman, acceptance is good, rejection is evil. Poetry should be inclusive, not exclusive. Even the old ideas of right and wrong no longer restrict the poet. He embraces and loves all. "Little or big, learned or unlearned, white or black, legal or illegal, sick or well, from the first inspiration down the windpipe to the last expiration out of it, all that a male or female does that is vigorous and benevolent and clean is so much sure profit to him or her in the unshakable order of the universe and through the whole scope of it together."

Certainly Whitman has the courage to use the license he demands for the poet. His poems in *Leaves of Grass* are concrete examples of his doctrines. No subject matter is unworthy. The factories, the docks, the plains, the mountains are listed along with every type of man and woman: the workers, the wives, the magistrates, the prostitutes. He uses a free-flowing rhythm that usually has neither rhyme nor meter in the old sense. Nor does he hesitate to use the diction that is spoken on the streets as well as that used in the courts.

We are as far as we can get from Horace and Boileau.

BIBLIOGRAPHY

Allen, G. W. *The Solitary Singer: a Critical Biography of Walt Whitman.* New York, 1955.
―――. *Walt Whitman as Man, Poet, and Legend.* With a Check List of Whitman Publications, 1945–1960, by E. A. Allen. Carbondale, 1961.
Arvin, Newton. *Whitman.* New York, 1938.
Canby, H. S. *Classic American.* New York, 1931.
Chase, R. V. *Walt Whitman.* Minneapolis, 1961.
Holloway, Emory. *Whitman: an Interpretation in Narrative.* New York, 1926.
Johnson, M. O. *Walt Whitman as a Critic of Literature.* Lincoln, 1938.
Metzger, C. R. *Thoreau and Whitman: a Study of Their Esthetics.* Seattle, 1961.
Sélincourt, Basil de. *Walt Whitman: a Critical Study.* London, 1914.
Traubel, Horace. *With Walt Whitman in Camden.* 3 vols. New York, 1906–1914.
Whitman, Walt. *The Complete Writings of;* ed. by R. M. Bucke, T. B. Harned, H. L. Traubel, and O. L. Triggs. 10 vols. New York, 1910.
―――. *The Collected Writings of;* ed. by G. W. Allen and Sculley Bradley. 15 vols. New York, 1961 (in progress).

18 · Sainte-Beuve (1804–1869)

THE ROMANTICS rejected the old standards of criticism. Some of them, like Hugo, attempted to set up new standards in their place. Yet the time had come when a critic would appear who would feel all abstract standards, new or old, too restraining. When he came his name was Charles-Augustin Sainte-Beuve.

For those whose preference is for aesthetics and metaphysics, Sainte-Beuve is no critic at all. For others he is the most completely satisfying critic who ever wrote. What Sainte-Beuve tried to do was to claim that his own taste and judgment gave him the right to evaluate literature. He is the teacher of literature par excellence. Starting with the writers or the literary works, rather than with theories, he tells us what they mean to him. They may not mean exactly the same to us, but he enriches our own experience of them by letting us see them through his eyes. The student does not always have to agree with his professor, but the good professor will enable him to see more clearly than he did before.

Yet to say that Sainte-Beuve has no theories is not to say that he has no methods. His critical life is a search for new and more useful ways of looking at literature. Starting out as a young Romantic of the Hugo group, he is at first filled with the spirit of protest against the old standards. As he develops he comes to see that the study of the critic is first to understand the writer before he begins to judge him.

Belonging to his own highly individualistic age, Sainte-Beuve naturally felt that the best way to understand a piece of literature was to find out about, and thus understand, the individual who wrote it.

As early as 1829 he could declare in the preface to Hugo's *Les Orientales*, "There are in poetry no good and no bad subjects, there are only good and bad poets." As physics was *the* science in the seventeenth century, and the "laws" of nature and the "rules" were part of the same world view, so biology is the leading science in the nineteenth century. Sainte-Beuve is the biologist, or if we prefer, the psychologist of literature. Thus, in trying to understand an author he will look at his grandparents and his parents, his brothers and sisters as well as the age he lived in. He recognized, of course, that the concept of the "age" or the "period" was a very useful one for the student of literature, but he refused to limit himself to this approach alone. Speaking of Taine, the environmental critic, Sainte-Beuve says: "Something still eludes him, the most vital part of man eludes him, which is the reason why out of twenty men, or a hundred or a thousand, apparently subject to almost the same intrinsic or external conditions, not one resembles the other, and there is one among them all who excels through originality." (*New Monday Chats*, viii, 1884)

So in a sense, he offers us a new science, the science of genius. Yet it is one that takes genius to practice. Criticism is in fact an art, and the critic who would be successful at it must be an artist. Sainte-Beuve looks at the writer not as an isolated individual but as a member of a group. "I define the group," he says, "not as the accidental and artificial assemblage of clever men who agree on an end, but the natural and spontaneous association of young minds and young talents, not exactly similar nor of the same family but of the same *flight*, and the same *Spring*, hatched under the same star, who feel themselves born, with varieties of taste and vocation, for a common work." (*Monday Chats*, 1861)

Any criticism that can content itself with one point of view, one set of theories, is too easy, and to be easy is to be false. Literature and the production of literature are most complex matters. So Sainte-Beuve asks more of the critic than any of his predecessors have done. He demands that the critic make the

author come to life. As he says in an article on Corneille in his
Monday Chats:

> It seems to me that, as regards the literary critic, there is no
> reading more recreative, more delectable, and at the same time more
> fruitful in all kinds of information than well-made biographies
> of great men. . . . To get inside one's author, to establish oneself
> there, to exhibit him from all points of view; to make him live,
> move and speak as he must have done, to follow him as far as pos-
> sible into his inner life and private manners; to tie him on all sides
> to this earth, this real existence, these daily habits which are as
> much a part of great men as the rest of us.

No scientist has a job more exacting than the job the critic
must perform. But to be a searcher out of facts is not enough.
The critic must re-create them, and to do so he needs the artistic ability of the poet. All that the scientist has, all the poet
has—this Sainte-Beuve demands that the critic have.

Though some of his judgments have to be revised, it is remarkable how well Sainte-Beuve performed his self-imposed
task. His *History of Port-Royal, Chateaubriand and His Literary
Group,* and his *Monday Chats* are still exciting to the lover of
literature. In these he continues the tradition of practical criticism that glimmers in Longinus and floods the pages of Dryden.
Literary theory is no longer considered in a vacuum. Whether
we agree or disagree with Sainte-Beuve, he offers us the concrete examples with which to test his judgment and exercise
our own. Let him be read on Rabelais and then on Rousseau,
two figures as unlike as possible, to appreciate his catholicity of
sympathy and his extraordinary skill in making the reader live
with the people he is writing about.

This ability to re-create personalities of all ages and temperaments does not result in complete relativism. In a lecture given
at the Ecole Normale, on April 12, 1858, Sainte-Beuve states
the position he has arrived at later in his life. He has wearied
of the Romantic enthusiasm of his youth and now prefers classic
literature. He follows Goethe's "by classic I understand sound
and by romantic sickly." He defines classic literature as com-
prising "all literatures in a healthy and happily flourishing condition, literatures in full accord and in harmony with their

period, with their social surroundings, with the principles and powers which direct society, satisfied with themselves . . . these literatures which are and feel themselves to be at home, in their proper road, not out of their proper class, not agitating, not having for their principle discomfort, which has never been a principle of beauty." (A *Literary Tradition*, 1858) Romantic literature on the other hand springs from ages which are in "a perpetual instability of public affairs." (*ibid.*) Since the writers of a romantic age find it difficult to believe in literary immortality, they permit themselves every license.

Though Sainte-Beuve expresses his personal preference for the literature of such stable ages as those of Pericles, Augustus, and Louis XIV, he cannot speak evil of the romantic literatures. He knows that writers do not choose the age they are born in and must do their best with their environment.

Having his own preferences, he is willing to allow others to have theirs, but he is sure that there is more real agreement among judges of literature than one might think. As he says, "I have often remarked that when two good intellects pass totally different judgments on the same author we may safely wager that it is because they are not, in fact, fixing their thoughts for the moment on the same object, on the same work of the author in question, on the same passages of his work; that it is because they have not the whole of him before their eyes, that they are not for the moment taking him in entirely. A closer attention, a wider knowledge, will bring together differing judgments and restore them to harmony. But even in the regular graduated circle of lawful admiration a certain latitude must be allowed to the diversity of tastes, minds, and ages. . . ." (*ibid.*)

BIBLIOGRAPHY

Babbitt, Irving. *Masters of Modern French Criticism*. Boston, 1912.
Billy, André. *Sainte-Beuve, sa vie et son temps*. Paris, 1952.

Bonnerot, Jean. *Un Demi-siècle d'études sur Sainte-Beuve, 1904–1954.* Paris, 1957.

Brunetière, Ferdinand. *L'Evolution des genres: la critique.* Paris, 1890.

Dowden, Edward. *New Studies in Literature.* Boston, 1895.

France, Anatole. *Préface aux poésies complètes de Sainte-Beuve.* Paris, 1879.

Giese, W. F. *Sainte-Beuve, a Literary Portrait.* Madison, 1931.

Guérard, A. L. *French Prophets of Yesterday.* London and New York, 1913.

Harper, G. M. *Charles-Augustin Sainte-Beuve.* Philadelphia, 1909.

Lehmann, A. G. *Sainte-Beuve. A Portrait of the Critic, 1806–1842.* Oxford, 1962.

MacClintock, Lander. *Sainte-Beuve's Critical Theory and Practice After 1849.* Chicago, 1920.

Michaut, G. M. *Sainte-Beuve.* Paris, 1921.

More, P. E. *Shelburne Essays.* New York, 1906.

Sainte-Beuve, C.-A. *Essays;* tr. with an introd. by Elizabeth Lee. London, 1892.

———. *Monday Chats;* Selected and tr. from *Causeries du lundi,* with an introd. by William Matthews. Chicago, 1877.

———. *Portraits of the Seventeenth Century, Historic and Literary;* tr. by K. P. Wormeley. New York, 1925.

———. *Portraits of the Eighteenth Century, Historic and Literary;* tr. by K. P. Wormeley, with a critical introd. by Edmond Scherer. New York, 1925.

———. *Selected Essays;* with introd., bibliography, and notes; ed. by J. R. Effinger, Jr. Boston, 1895.

19 · Taine (1828–1893)

SOME MEN do not want freedom. They are uncomfortable in the face of that diversity in which Sainte-Beuve rejoiced. Everything must be explained, must be fitted into a pattern, or they find life unliveable.

Such a man was Hippolyte Adolphe Taine. An admirer of Sainte-Beuve, he found that Sainte-Beuve's method was, at least for him, not enough. He desired a degree of certainty that Sainte-Beuve could not give him. At the time he wrote, however, it was impossible for him to turn back to the absolutes of an earlier generation, but, living in the scientific and sociological atmosphere of the middle nineteenth century, he believed that he could substitute new scientific "truths" about literature for the old ones. In the preface to his *Essays*, he says, "A scope similar to that of the natural sciences is open to the moral sciences. . . . History, the latest comer, can discover laws like its elders have."

His own personality must also be taken into account. The easier optimism of an earlier period was not for him. The hope of the revolutionists of 1789, 1830, and 1848, the belief in the goodness and perfectability of man, had ended in—Napoleon III. He could not view human nature except from a pessimistic viewpoint. One must be realistic.

In his introduction to his *History of English Literature* (1864), Taine explains his new, scientific approach to literature. "It was perceived that a literary work is not a mere individual play of imagination, the isolated caprice of an excited brain, but a transcript of contemporary manners, a manifestation of a certain kind of mind. It was concluded that we might recover, from the monuments of literature, a knowledge of the manner in which men thought and felt centuries ago. The attempt was made, and it succeeded."

Determined to be scientific, Taine decides to approach literature in much the same way as the biologist approaches his specimen. A literary document is like a fossil shell. It bears the imprint of the organism that lived in it. "Under the shell there was an animal, and behind the document there was a man." Both the document and the shell are lifeless, but both may be examined as clues to living existences. It would be a mistake to study them as if they were isolated. "Neither mythology nor languages exist in themselves; but only men, who arrange words and imagery according to the necessities of their organs and the original bent of their intellects." The methods of the biological sciences can be applied to literature.

Since behind each book there is a man, we must first consider him. But looking merely at his face, his clothes, and his actions is not enough. We must penetrate to that "mass of faculties and feelings" which are the inner man. After we have laid bare this inner man and have worked out his psychology, we have done what has been done by no one "so justly and grandly as Sainte-Beuve." But we cannot stop here. We must, now that we have collected the facts, search out the causes. "No matter if the facts be physical, or moral, they all have their causes; there is a cause for ambition, for courage, for truth as there is for digestion, for muscular movement, for animal heat. Vice and virtue are products like vitriol and sugar; and every complex phenomenon arises from other more simple phenomenon on which it hangs."

Looking closely, we discover that there is a system in human ideas and sentiments, and that "this system has for its native power certain general traits, certain characteristics of the intellect and the heart common to the men of one race or country. As in mineralogy, the crystals, however diverse, spring from certain simple physical forms, so in history, civilizations, however diverse, are derived from certain simple spiritual forms."

In each man we are able to find an elementary moral state which is not complex, and from this we can see the outline in which civilizations are constrained to exist. There are three sources for this elementary moral state: RACE, SURROUNDINGS, and EPOCH.

RACE. For this concept, Taine has unfortunately to rely on the shaky anthropology of the mid-nineteenth century. At this time, language and race were confused in a way that is now considered naïve. The great Indo-European language group which contains the major European languages as well as Sanskrit and Persian was held to be the language of one race, the Aryan. Believing this, Taine could assert that the ancient Greeks and most of the modern Europeans have in common a mental structure which makes them differ from the Chinese and the Semites.

SURROUNDINGS. Yet, obviously, there is a difference in the literature of, say the Scots and the Italians even if both are considered to be Aryans. This results from the differences of their environments. "For man is not alone in the world; nature surrounds him and his fellowmen surround him, accidental and secondary tendencies overlay his primitive tendencies." Climate, for instance, has an effect. "The gloomy mists of the north produce one sort of society; the bright and sunny coasts of the south another."

EPOCH. There is a third cause. A Frenchman of the twelfth century does not have the same dominant ideas as a Frenchman of the seventeenth. So, the time, the epoch, must be considered, too.

These are the three sources. Taine says that by using them we can not only understand past literatures but predict future creations.

So much we can say with confidence that the unknown creations towards which the current of the centuries conducts will be raised up and regulated together by the three primordial forces; that if these forces could be measured and computed, we might deduce from them as from a formula the characteristics of future civilization. . . . For, in enumeration of them, we traverse the complete circle of the agencies; and when we have considered Race, Surroundings, and Epoch, which are the internal mainsprings, the external pressure, and the acquired momentum, we have exhausted not only the whole of the actual causes, but also the whole of the possible causes of motion.

Taine now has to his own satisfaction arrived at the point where one can once more talk about literature as a whole. To be sure, his interest in literature is not so much in the literature itself as in what can be learned from literary documents. "A great poem, a fine novel, the confessions of a superior man, are more instructive than a heap of historians with their histories . . . they are instructive because they are beautiful; their utility grows with their perfection, and if they furnish documents it is because they are monuments."

So primarily we study literature so that we can construct a moral history and advance toward an understanding of the laws of psychology. Though Taine subordinates literature to sociology, his method deeply influenced the study of literature and the writing of literary history in particular.

BIBLIOGRAPHY

Babbitt, Irving. *Masters of Modern French Critics.* Boston, 1912.

Chevrillon, André. *Taine: Formation de sa pensée.* Paris, 1932.

Clark, H. H. *The Influence of Science on American Literary Criticism, 1860–1910, Including the Vogue of Taine.* Madison, 1956.

Eustis, A. A. *Hippolyte Taine and the Classical Genius.* Berkeley, 1951.

Gummere, F. B. *Democracy and Poetry.* Boston, 1911.

Hardison, O. B., ed. *Modern Continental Literary Criticism.* New York, 1962.

Kahn, S. J. *Science and Aesthetic Judgment; a Study in Taine's Critical Method.* New York, 1953.

Monod, Gabriel J. J. *Les Maîtres de l'histoire: Renan, Taine, Michelet.* Paris, 1896.

Taine, H. A. *Lectures on Art;* tr. by John Durand. New York, 1877.

———. *History of English Literature;* tr. by H. Van Laun. Edinburgh, 1873.

20 · Matthew Arnold (1822–1888)

ARNOLD LOOKED around at mid-nineteenth-century England and did not like what he saw. Industrial progress there was, but moral grandeur was lacking. From a cultural point of view most of the aristocrats were "barbarians," the middle-class "Philistines," and the people a brutalized "populace."

Yet this view of the world could not lead this Englishman to Taine's deep pessimism. On the contrary. Arnold felt that the duty of the critic was to prepare an atmosphere that would stimulate the artist and bring home to the people a knowledge of the best literature. So, although one of the key words in his criticism is "disinterestedness," he does not mean by it an art-for-art's-sake attitude. The critic must be disinterested, not because he has no social function, but because he has one.

In his essay "The Function of Criticism at the Present Time" he makes this abundantly clear. The critic must keep himself aloof from the "practical view of things." He must not lend himself to mere political and practical considerations. There is, to the shame of England, more than enough of this kind of criticism. The main critical organs are subservient to practical ends. The *Edinburgh Review* looks at everything from the point of view of the Whigs, the *Quarterly Review* from the point of view of the Tories, and *The Times* from the point of view of the "common, satisfied, well-to-do Englishman."

True criticism must be independent of these interests, or it will never attain real authority or perform its function of creating "a current of true and fresh ideas." Directly polemical and controversial criticism has a record of failure. The rush of practical life will always make the spectators dizzy. Only the critic who remains collected and refuses to be practical can do the practical man a service. Without disinterestedness there is no possibility of truth and high culture. A high culture will come about only when the critic has prepared the way for the poet.

In his "Study of Poetry," Arnold claims the highest future for poetry. "The future of poetry," he writes, "is immense, because in poetry where it is worthy of its high destinies, our race, as time goes on, will find an ever surer and surer stay. There is not a creed which is not shaken, not an accredited dogma which is not shown to be questionable, not a received tradition which does not threaten to dissolve. Our religion has materialized itself in the fact, and now the fact is failing it. But for poetry the idea is everything; the rest is a world of illusion, of divine illusion. Poetry attaches its emotion to the idea, the idea *is* the fact. The strongest part of our religion today is its unconscious poetry."

We have seen many noble things claimed for poetry by critics in the past, but Arnold claims more than any of them. The battle for men's minds that is being waged by science and religion will be won by neither. Religion and philosophy, the "shadows and dreams and false shows of knowledge," will be replaced by poetry. Science itself will be completed by it. As Wordsworth said, "poetry will be the breath and finer spirit of all knowledge."

If poetry is to have this supremely high place, the standards set for it must be equally high. The poetry in which the spirit of the people will find its "consolation and stay" must be "excellent," "sound," and "true." In other words only the best poetry can be admitted. This "will be found to have a power of forming, sustaining, and delighting us as nothing else can."

How can we find this poetry? First, says Arnold, "neither the historical or the personal approach will aid us. Both approaches are fallacious since both are liable to make us praise or dispraise for reasons that have nothing to do with poetry." Taine, Sainte-Beuve, and a host of other critics, are brushed aside.

We must have objective, not historical or personal, standards. We must, in other words, have a measuring stick. "Indeed there can be no more useful help for discovering what poetry belongs to the class of the truly excellent, and can do us most good, than to have always in one's mind lines and expressions of the great masters, and to apply them as a touchstone to other poetry." If we keep lines of high poetic quality in our minds they will be infallible touchstones for detecting the presence or absence of high poetic quality.

As examples Arnold gives lines from Homer, Dante, Shakespeare, and Milton. He forgets that he has told us in earlier essays that the highest poetic quality depends on selection and arrangement and offers his touchstones of a line or two as all that is necessary. "These few lines, if we have tact and can use them, are enough even of themselves to keep clear and sound our judgments about poetry, to save us from fallacious estimates of it, to conduct us to a real estimate."

Most readers will feel that Arnold has let himself be carried away. The lines he quotes from Hamlet's dying request to Horatio:

> If thou didst ever hold me in thy heart,
> Absent thee from felicity awhile,
> And in this harsh world draw thy breath in pain
> To tell my story . . . .

are admired by all, but does not a large part of this admiration depend on the fact that we know everything that leads up to them? Is it not wrong to demand as much from a few lines as Arnold does? Indeed, it is doubtful if anyone could feel what Arnold wants us to feel from the lines of Milton:

> And courage never to submit or yield
> And what is else not to be overcome.

Apart from the context any poetic quality in those lines is difficult to discover, certainly not the "very highest poetic quality."

With his taste for the classics, his relative blindness to later literature, and his desire for standards without being able to accept the old neoclassical rules, Arnold was forced to find something more concrete than an abstract expression of his preferences. It is a challenge he was brave enough to meet, and we can admire his courage even though we are forced to find his touchstones inadequate.

Arnold's elevation of poetry to a higher rank than religion, philosophy, and science makes him very jealous of the amount of poetry he will admit to the highest position. The best poetry, he says, must possess "in the eminent degree, truth and seriousness." Poetry that does not have high seriousness is not truly great. By high seriousness he means a moral excellence which is congruent with his own morality. Thus he denies Chaucer a place in the first rank and complains of Burns because of his "Scotch drink, Scotch religion, and Scotch manners."

What Arnold likes we like, but we will not always limit ourselves as he does, because we cannot help but feel that he narrowed poetry in attempting to exalt it. Yet, if poetry was to be a substitute for religion, he could do no other. And he has had followers. Such American critics as Irving Babbitt and Paul Elmer More in the twentieth century preached much the same doctrine as Arnold's under the title of the "New Humanism."

BIBLIOGRAPHY

Arnold, Matthew. *Essays in Criticism. First and Second Series Complete.* New York, 1902.
———. *Essays in Criticism.* 3rd Series. Boston, 1910.
———. *Essays, Letters and Reviews;* collected and ed. by Fraser Neiman. Cambridge, 1960.
Buckley, Vincent. *Poetry and Morality; Studies on the Criticism of Matthew Arnold, T. S. Eliot, and F. R. Leavis.* With an introd. by Basil Willey. London, 1959.
Dawson, W. H. *Matthew Arnold and His Relation to the Thought of Our Time.* New York, 1904.
Eells, J. S. *The Touchstones of Matthew Arnold.* New York, 1955.
Garrod, H. W. *Poetry and the Criticism of Life.* Cambridge, 1931.
Harvey, C. H. *Matthew Arnold. A Critic of the Victorian Period.* London, 1931.

James, D. G. *Matthew Arnold and the Decline of English Romanticism*. Oxford, 1961.

James, Henry. *Views and Reviews*. Boston, 1908.

Kelman, John. *Prophets of Yesterday and Their Message for Today*. Cambridge, 1924.

Kelso, A. P. *Matthew Arnold on Continental Life and Literature*. Oxford, 1914.

Orrick, N. B. *Matthew Arnold and Goethe*. London, 1928.

Renwanz, Johannes. *Matthew Arnold und Deutschland*. Griefswald, 1927.

Sells, I. E. *Matthew Arnold and France*. New York, 1935.

Shafer, Robert. *Christianity and Naturalism; Essays in Criticism*. New Haven, 1926.

Sherman, S. P. *Matthew Arnold, How to Know Him*. Indianapolis, 1917.

Trilling, Lionel. *Matthew Arnold*. New York, 1939.

21 · William Dean Howells (1837–1920)

NO GREATER CONTRAST to Arnold could be imagined than the American William Dean Howells. Arnold loves the past, is a student of the classics; Howells finds that almost every classic "is as dead as the people who wrote it." Arnold has little sympathy with contemporary literature. Howells is the encourager of the new, the defender of Hamlin Garland, Stephen Crane, and Frank Norris. Reality takes away from art, according to Arnold; reality is the test of art, according to Howells.

In an essay on Tolstoy, Arnold writes: "The truth is we are not to take *Anna Karenina* as a work of art; we are to take it as a piece of life. A piece of life it is. That author has not invented and combined it, he has seen it; it has happened before his inward eye, and it was in this wise that it happened. . . . The author saw it all happening so—saw it, and therefore relates it; and what his novel in this way loses in art, it gains in reality."

Again, nothing could be farther from Howells. For this American, reality can never hurt art. Thus it is that his remarks on Tolstoy become a refutation of Arnold's. "If Tolstoy had represented the past truly, as in his conscience and intelligence he had known it really to be, he had treated it ethically and of necessity aesthetically; for as you cannot fail to feel in every piece of his fiction, the perfect aesthetics result from the perfect ethics. . . ."

Howells joins hands with his fellow countryman Whitman in rejecting much of the old literature because it lacks a democratic spirit. Scott is condemned because of his "medieval ideals, his blind Jacobitism, for his intense devotion to aristocracy and royalty." For Howells the old classical attitudes are largely a product of the aristocratic way of looking at things.

His *Criticism and Fiction* (1891) is an attack on what he calls the "vested interests of criticism." Art is nothing but the expression of life and cannot be judged by any other standard than its truth to life. The traditional critics have browbeaten those with wholesome common sense into accepting their false lights. Since fidelity to life is the test of art, the common people can judge of art as well, if not better, than the critics. They have not done so because they "have been afraid to apply their own simplicity, naturalness, and honesty to the appreciation of the beautiful." But the time is coming, he hopes, when the average man will have the courage to apply his own standards; when that time comes the old order of critics who have the intellectual mission of representing the "petrifications of taste" and preserving "an image of a smaller and cruder and emptier world than we now live in" will no longer be listened to.

No critic is an authority. No author was ever an authority "except in those moments when he held his ear close to nature's lips and caught its very accent." The best art is the art which is the most realistic. At the beginning of the nineteenth century, Romanticism fought with effete classicism. At the end of the nineteenth century, realism is waging the same battle with effete Romanticism.

The true realist is one who finds nothing in life insignificant, who will not feel that there is anything unworthy or beneath his notice, but who "feels in every nerve the equality of things and the unity of men; his soul is exalted, not by vain shows and shadows and ideals, but by realities, in which alone the truth lives." Grown men cannot remain content with "Jack the Giant Killer," "Puss in Boots," or Balzac's "Sworn Thirteen Noblemen."

Howells defines realism as "nothing more and nothing less than the truthful treatment of material. . . ." Applying this standard to the English novelists, only Jane Austen measures up completely. The history of the English novel from Jane Austen through Scott, Dickens, Charlotte Brontë, and Thackeray is the history of a decline, a decline attributable to the false and perverted taste of the English, a taste for which the critics have no little responsibility.

In America the situation is different. This country has been built upon the affirmation that all men are equal in their rights and their duties. The American novelists should be "as American as they unconsciously can." For if they put aside all the false ideals of effete classicism and effete Romanticism—and, at the same time, do not become mere propagandists—they will be able to make American art truly democratic.

Matthew Arnold complains that American life has no "distinction." This is its very virtue, says Howells. The American should portray the "common beauty, common grandeur, or the beauty and grandeur in which the quality of solidarity so prevails that neither distinguishes itself to the disadvantage of anything else." This will make for true "distinction," not the false "distinction" of Arnold. The American novelist must be democratic and realistic. Having demanded fidelity to life, Howells finds himself embarrassed by the question of whether the American novelist should deal with those "facts of life" which are not talked about in nineteenth-century Boston's polite society. He greatly admires the European realists who deal with such matters with great freedom, but at the same time he respects the propriety, or if you will the prudery, of his time. He defends it by pointing out that the Anglo-Saxon novelist is no more shut up in his "tradition of decency" than the continental novelist in his "tradition of indecency." Is not the Anglo-Saxon tradition the more realistic if we look at it closely? "The manners of the novel have been improving with those of its readers; that is all. Gentlemen no longer swear or fall drunk under the table, or abduct young ladies and shut them up in lonely country houses, or so habitually set about the ruin of their neighbor's wives, as they once did. Generally, people now call a spade an agricultural implement. . . ."

So be it. Howells is willing to accept what he calls the "scientific decorum" of his society. Yet he by no means suggests that the novelist should concern himself only with the pleasant aspects of American life. On the contrary, he proclaims that art will perish if it does not concern itself with the victims of society. "Truth . . . paints these victims as they are, and bids the world consider them not because they are beautiful and virtuous, but because they are ugly and vicious, cruel, filthy, and only not altogether loathsome because the divine can never wholly die out of the human." Truth must also paint those other victims of society, the aimless, satiated, selfish rich.

Howells is a humanitarian and a socialist. The art of fiction is a finer art than it has been before because it is more realistic, and being more realistic is more useful. Perhaps the time will come when even the story, the fable, will be considered foolish. Then fiction may be "superseded by a still more faithful form of contemporaneous history." A good television documentary would have greatly pleased him if he had lived to see it.

Art for art's sake has no place in life. The aristocratic spirit which is disappearing from politics and society, has found refuge in aesthetics. "The pride of caste is becoming the pride of taste."

But, concludes Howells, "Democracy in literature is the reverse of all this. . . . Neither arts, nor letters, nor sciences, except as they somehow, clearly or obscurely, tend to make the race better and kinder, are to be regarded as serious interests; they are all lower than the rudest crafts that feed and house and clothe, for except they do this office they are idle; and they cannot do this except from and through the truth."

BIBLIOGRAPHY

Bennett, G. N. *William Dean Howells: the Development of a Novelist*. Norman, 1959.

Brooks, Van Wyck. *Howells, His Life and World*. New York, 1959.

Cady, E. H. *The Realist at War: the Mature Years, 1885–1920, of William Dean Howells*. Syracuse, 1958.

Cooke, D. G. *William Dean Howells*. New York, 1922.

De Mille, G. E. *Literary Criticism in America*. New York, 1931.

Eble, K. E. *Howells: a Century of Criticism*. Dallas, 1962.

Firkins, O. W. *William Dean Howells*. Cambridge, 1924.

Gibson, W. M., and George Arms. *A Bibliography of William Dean Howells*. New York, 1948.

Howells, William Dean. *Criticism and Fiction, and Other Essays*; ed. by Clara M. Kirk and Rudolf Kirk. New York, 1959.

Trent, W. P. *The Authority of Criticism*. New York, 1899.

Wilkinson, W. C. *Some New Literary Valuations*. New York, 1909.

22 · Emile Zola (1840–1902)

THE NAME of Emile Zola is connected, thanks both to his novels and to his criticism, with the term "naturalism." In its broadest sense, naturalism means nothing more than the return of art, particularly the novel, to nature. Since Howells defined realism as, in essence, the truthful treatment of life, naturalism and realism seem, at first glance, to be the same thing. Certainly naturalism is a form of realism, but is it anything more?

For Zola it is. Naturalism is, he might say, scientific realism. It is realism which accepts and uses the scientific method. It is further based upon the proposition that man's free will is an illusion and his acts are determined by his heredity and environment. This emphasis on determinism distinguishes Zola's naturalism from other forms of realism.

His theory is given in its clearest and its most extreme form in his essay "The Experimental Novel" (1880). Here he boldly advances the thesis that literature should be governed by the same scientific method that governs the natural sciences. "I am going to try and prove that if the experimental method leads to the knowledge of physical life, it should also lead to the knowledge of the passionate and intellectual life. It is but a question of degree in the same path which runs from chemistry to physiology, then from physiology to anthropology and to sociology. The experimental novel is the goal."

He feels that all he needs to do to create the scientific novel is to employ the experimental method laid down by Claude Bernard in his *Introduction to the Study of Experimental Medicine*. This famous doctor warns against hit-or-miss empiricism or any medical "doctrine" or philosophical "system." Experimental science never worries about the "why" of things; it is content to explain the "how." Bernard insists that living bodies are as absolutely determined by natural phenomena as inanimate bodies. Thus the "provoked observation," which is the name he gives to experiment, is equally applicable to both.

Bernard, states Zola, makes an important distinction between the "observer" and the "experimentalist." The observer merely describes the phenomena under his eyes. The experimentalist has a hypothesis or preconceived idea. He then conducts an experiment to confirm or refute this idea. After this he must transform himself into an observer in order to judge impartially whether his preconceived idea is proved or disproved by the results.

This method, says Zola, is applicable to the novel. The novelist is both an observer and an experimentalist. Like the observer, he gives the facts as he sees them. "Then the experimentalist appears and introduces an experiment, that is to say, sets his characters going in a certain story so as to show that the succession of facts will be such as the requirements of the determinism of the phenomena under examination call for." Zola asserts that Balzac does this in his *Cousine Bette*. Balzac has observed what happens to a man's home and his place in society if he has an amorous temperament. He makes his experiment by exposing his character, Baron Hulot, to a series of trials. This, says Zola, is experimentation, since Balzac "does not remain satisfied with photographing the facts collected by him, but interferes in a direct way to place his characters in certain conditions, and of these he remains the master." Thus Balzac works out the problem of what such a passion, acting in such and such circumstances, will produce. Employing such a method, says Zola, "enables you to possess knowledge of the man, scientific knowledge of him, in both his individual and social relations." Then, he continues, "It is undeniable that the naturalistic novel, as we understand it today, is a real experiment that a novelist makes on man by the help of observation."

Zola feels that the experimental method is the answer to those critics who complain that naturalistic novelists are mere photographers. The very idea of experimentation implies that the novelist does more than merely reproduce facts. For, "to show the mechanism of these facts, it is necessary for us to produce and direct the phenomena; this is our share of invention, here is the genius in the book."

Yet Claude Bernard himself will not accept the artist as scientist. He defines him as "a man who realizes in a work of art an idea or a sentiment which is personal to him." Everything Zola has said will be meaningless if he accepts Bernard's objection, so naturally he refuses to do so. Zola argues that the personality of the artist is subordinate to truth and nature and that the artist no more allows his personality to interfere with his experiment than the scientist in the laboratory does his.

Thus the artist and the scientist are the same. The artist must know the discoveries of science so that he can adopt them and build his own scientific novel on the solid basis of proven hypotheses. The only area where the writer may risk hypotheses is in the area where the facts are not yet settled. "The experimental novelist is therefore the one who accepts proven facts, who points out in man and in society the mechanism of the phenomena over which science is mistress, and who does not interpose his personal sentiments, except in the phenomena whose determinism is not yet settled, and who tries to test, as much as he can, this personal sentiment, this idea *a priori*, by observation and experiment."

Zola is convinced that the experimental method will triumph everywhere, not only in the novel but in history, criticism, the drama, and even poetry, since literature depends not only upon the author but upon nature.

The metaphysical man is dead; our whole territory is transformed by the advent of the physiological man. No doubt "Achilles' Anger," and "Dido's Love," will last forever on account of their beauty; but today we feel the necessity of analyzing anger and love, of discovering how such passions work in the human being. . . . In short, everything is summed up in this great fact; the experimental method in letters, as in the sciences, is in the way to explain the natural phenomena, both individual and social, of which metaphysics, until now, has given only irrational and supernatural explanations.

Thus spoke Zola. The influence of science on nineteenth-century critical thinking had become so powerful that we find this novelist denying that literature is separate from the sciences. It is, if experimental, a science itself.

If Zola had merely contended that the novelist must document, must use advances in science, must attempt to be truthful in the sense that he portrays his characters as doing what he honestly thinks they would do in certain circumstances, he would have protected himself from his critics. But he exaggerates to the point where his position becomes nonsensical. It is' self-evident that the writer cannot experiment in the way the physiologist can. Both characters and situations are the products of his "invention" no matter how well he documents them, and this fact alone disposes of any real experimentation in the laboratory sense. To be a truly experimental novelist he would have to experiment upon living human beings. If he did, his experiment would soon be cut short by the arrival of the police.

BIBLIOGRAPHY

Carrère, Jean. *Degeneration in the Great French Masters*. London, 1922.

Croce, Benedetto. *European Literature in the Nineteenth Century*. New York, 1924.

Doucet, F. *L'Esthétique de Zola et son application à la critique*. La Haye, 1923.

Ellis, Havelock. *Affirmations*. London, 1898.

Frye, F. H. *Literary Reviews and Criticisms*. New York, 1908.

Hemmings, F. W. *Emile Zola*. Oxford, 1953.

James, Henry. *Notes on Novelists*. New York, 1914.

Josephson, Matthew. *Zola and His Time*. New York, 1928.

Root, W. H. *German Criticism of Zola*. New York, 1931.

Tolstoy, Count Leo. *Emile Zola, Novelist and Reformer*. London, 1904.

Zola, Emile. *The Experimental Novel and Other Essays*; tr. by Belle M. Sherman. New York, 1893.

23 · Anatole France (1844–1924)

SOME MEN are skeptical of religion, others of politics, others of economics. Few are skeptical of everything. Of these few was Anatole France. Even literature, the field in which he labored and which he loved, was subjected by him to a critique that attempted to destroy all standards of either tradition or taste. France declared that no critic can do more than speak for himself when he pretends to speak of literary works. The honest critic will, then, call his literary criticism the "adventures of his soul among the masterpieces" and make no pretense to objectivity. This kind of criticism has been called impressionistic in the sense that only subjective impressions are offered.

Again and again Anatole France repeats that if a critic claims to be objective, he is merely deluding his readers and himself. In his preface to the fourth series of *Life and Letters* (1889) he vigorously attacks each and every school of criticism. Aesthetics, he argues, is the least exact of all branches of knowledge, a true castle in the air, because it has no solid base. Attempts to base aesthetic judgments on ethics, on sociology, and on science have been made and have failed for the simple reason that none of these fields has a firm foundation itself.

Other aestheticians speak glibly of tradition and universal consent. There are no such things. "The works that everyone admires are those that no one examines." Only those who first chose the classics were free. The rest of us merely follow their lead and exercise no judgment of any sort. You can prove this by taking a passage from a famous work. If you say it was written by an unknown, everyone will find it full of faults.

If you but say it is by Shakespeare, everyone will admire it. The famous aesthetician Victor Cousin praised as sublimities words in Pascal that were later discovered to have been printers' errors. Ossian was considered the equal of Homer when he was thought to be an ancient Celt. When it was discovered that his poem was by a modern, his virtues ceased to exist.

A very interesting work would be the history of the varying criticisms of one of those works to which humanity has paid the greatest attention: *Hamlet*, the *Divine Comedy* or the *Iliad*. The *Iliad* delights us today by a barbaric and primitive quality which many of us discover in it in all good faith. In the seventeenth century Homer was praised for having observed the rules of the epic.

"Be assured," said Boileau, "that if Homer has employed the word *dog* it is because that word is noble in Greek." These ideas are ridiculous to us. Ours will perhaps appear equally ridiculous in two hundred years' time, for after all we cannot rank the statements that Homer is barbaric and that barbarism is admirable among the eternal truths. In questions of literature there is not a single opinion that cannot easily be opposed by a contrary opinion. Who could ever terminate the disputes of the flute players?

Sympathetic as the skeptic within us is to France's attack on the self-satisfaction of pretentious absolutists, we suspect that he was deliberately exaggerating his position in order to shock us. No one who wrote as well as he could deny that deep within himself he made judgments of the same kind he scoffed at others for making.

BIBLIOGRAPHY

Axelrad, Jacob. *Anatole France, a Life Without Illusions, 1844–1924.* New York and London, 1944.

Belis, Alexandre. *La Critique française à la fin du XIXe siècle.* Paris, 1926.

Chevalier, H. M. *The Ironic Temper: Anatole France and His Time.* New York, 1932.

France, Anatole. *Œuvres complètes.* 25 vols. Paris, 1925–1932.

———. *On Life and Letters, 1st Series, 2nd and 3rd and 4th Series.* 3 vols. London, 1914–1924.

Thorold, A. L. *Six Masters in Disillusion.* London, 1909.

24 · Ferdinand Brunetière (1849–1906)

AGAINST both the naturalism of Zola and all relativism in literary criticism stood Ferdinand Brunetière. A defender of the Catholic church in religion and of conservatism in politics, he was temperamentally in favor of authority in literature. For him criticism that expressed the personality of the critic could not even be considered criticism. Nor could he accept the popular idea that literature was a form of sociology.

How, then, could he approach literature? He could, of course, have turned back to the neoclassical rules, but by the late nineteenth century that was hardly possible. So what he did was to borrow the theory of evolution from biology and apply it to literature. By so doing he was able to get back to authority while using the modern scientific method but without identifying literature with science. As he stated in the *Evolution of Genres* (1890):

> The theory of evolution must have had something in it which justified its good luck . . . . Since we know what Natural History, what History, what Philosophy have already got out of it, I would like to find out whether Literary History and Criticism is not also able to take advantage of it.

No more remarkable tribute to the dominance of the scientific method of thinking could be given than this. In order for Brunetière to attack the identification of literature with sociology and biology, in order to claim for literature its own laws as distinct from natural laws, he had to show that literary genres are like biological genres in that all are born, develop, and die like living beings. Who could have predicted that the

beloved genres of the neoclassicists would now come back under the protection of the theory of evolution? Yet this is what
happens in *The Evolution of Genres in the History of Literature*, which Brunetière published in 1890.

He considers that he is able to reestablish laws for each
type of literature that will not be, as were the neoclassical rules,
subject to the criticism that they are arbitrary. The laws Brunetière abstracts arise, he contends, from the nature of the literary forms themselves.

We can best illustrate his method by turning to his essay
"The Law of the Drama" which was published as a preface
to his *Annals of the Theatre and Music* in 1894. Being in search
of the true characteristic or law of the drama, he denies that
the old neoclassical rules are anything more than conventions
which vary according to the necessities of the play, the age
in which it is written, and the author. Corneille subordinates
character to situation, Racine subordinates situation to character. Either way works. Racine's subjects adjust themselves to
the three unities; Shakespeare's do not. "Evidently all these
alleged Rules effect or express only the most superficial characteristics of the drama."

But, says Brunetière, there is something which does not depend on these superficial characteristics. In other words, there
is a law of drama which can be discovered by analyzing dramas
of all the different schools. In each and every one of them, he
finds that the protagonist *wills* to do something. "Is it not
easy now to draw the conclusion? In drama or farce, what we
ask of the theatre is the spectacle of a *will* striving towards a
goal, and conscious of the means which it employs."

The novel is the exact opposite of the drama. *Gil Blas*, the
novel, and *The Marriage of Figaro*, the play, illustrate this.
Gil Blas has no goal, but Figaro wants a certain definite thing
and constantly wills what he wills. "The material or the subject of a novel or of a play may therefore be the same at bot-
tom; but they become drama or novel only by the manner in
which they are treated; and the manner is not merely different,
it is opposite."

This settled, Brunetière continues: "The same law provides,
further, the possibility of defining with precision the dramatic

species—about as one does the biologic species; and for that it is only necessary to consider the particular obstacle against which the will struggles."

If the obstacles are insurmountable, the will of the gods, the laws of nature, or the like, the result is *tragedy*.

If there is just one chance of victory over such obstacles as passion, prejudice, and the like, the result is *romantic drama* or *social drama*.

If the conditions of the struggle are changed, and two wills meet each other in apparently equal conditions, the result is *comedy*.

If the obstacle is located not in an opposing will but in the irony of fortune or in the disproportion between the means and the end, the result is *farce*.

In this manner Brunetière succeeds in reestablishing the old dramatic genres. He admits that admixtures occur but contends that these distinctions are useful since they may help authors avoid the error of treating a subject of comedy with the devices of farce, and so forth. "The general law of the theatre is defined by the action of a will conscious of itself; and the dramatic species are distinguished by the nature of the obstacles encountered by this will."

Using this law one can even evaluate the dramatic genres. The quality of will measures and determines dramatic value. Tragedy is superior to comedy and comedy to farce because "one drama is superior to another drama according as the quality of will exerted is greater or less, as the share of chance is less, and that of necessity greater." Thanks to the theory of evolution, the neoclassical hierarchy lives again.

The history of literature confirms this law, he continues. A nation has great dramatic art at the exact moment when the will of the people is most exalted. Greek tragedy is contemporary with the Persian wars. The great Spanish dramatists come at the time when Spain is extending her dominion throughout the Old and the New World. The great French drama comes hard at the heels of the mighty struggle that resulted in the unity of the French nation. To be sure, upsurges of national wills have taken place without a dramatic renaissance being the result, but no dramatic renaissance has come into being without being announced by some arousing of the people's will.

From this law other consequences seem to spring. In periods favorable to the drama the novel does not flourish, and the reverse is also true. The novel belongs to periods when the will is relaxed. "The Orientals have no drama, but they have novels. That is because they are fatalists, or determinists if you prefer, which amounts to the same thing, for today at least; and when the Greeks had a drama, they no longer had novels, I mean epics; they no longer had an *Odyssey*."

The law Brunetière establishes has moral consequences. A belief in freedom not only makes for drama but "is of no small assistance in the struggle that we undertake against the obstacles which prevent us from attaining our object." Thus his objection to the Zola school is moral as well as philosophical.

As a result of Brunetière's theory of genres, closer attention was henceforth paid to the influence on a writer's work of other works of the same class that had preceded it. Even those who could not accept his theory in its entirety found this a fruitful emphasis.

BIBLIOGRAPHY

Archer, William. *Playmaking*. New York, 1910.

Bondy, L.-J. *Le Classicisme de Ferdinand Brunetière*. Baltimore, 1930.

Brunetière, Ferdinand. *Art and Morality*; tr. with introd. by Arthur Beatty. New York, 1899.

———. *Etudes critiques sur l'histoire de la littérature française*. Paris, 1890.

———. *L'Evolution des genres dans l'histoire de la littérature*. Paris, 1890.

———. *Honoré de Balzac*; tr. by R. L. Sanderson. Philadelphia, 1906.

———. *Law of the Drama*; tr. by Philip M. Hayden. New York, 1914.

————. *Le Roman naturaliste.* New ed., Paris, 1893.

Giraud, Victor. *Brunetière.* Paris, 1932.

Hocking, Elton. *Ferdinand Brunetière: the Evolution of a Critic.* Madison, 1936.

Nonteuil, Jacques. *Ferdinand Brunetière.* Paris, 1933.

25 · Darwinism and Literature

BRUNETIÈRE's use of the catchword "evolution" reminds us that various theories of evolution influenced most thinkers of the nineteenth century, literary critics included. Yet, no literary critic quite dared become a complete neo-Darwinist since to become one would have meant supporting the proposition that literature became better as the race progressed. Regardless of how firm a man's belief in evolution was in other spheres, he could hardly claim that Browning was superior to Shakespeare because he was born roughly two hundred and fifty years later.

Nevertheless, Darwin deserves a place in any history of literary criticism since he influenced the content and form of nineteenth-century English literature to a greater degree than did any other scientist.

To appreciate his uniqueness, we have only to consider how slight the literary influence of an equally great scientist of our day, Einstein, has been. There are two reasons for this. First, Darwin worked in a field where his findings could be expressed in verbal instead of in mathematical symbols. Second, the concept of evolution was highly congenial to a society conscious of change and, indeed, was a popular literary theme before he formulated his theory of natural selection.

For such a poet as Tennyson, pre-Darwinian theories of evolution seemed to guarantee not only material but intellectual and ethical progress. In 1842, he could write in "Locksley Hall":

For I dipt into the future, far as human eye could see,
Saw the Vision of the world, and all the wonder that would be;

. . .
Eye, to which all order festers, all things here are out of joint:
Science moves, but slowly, slowly, creeping on from point to point:

. . .
Yet I doubt not thro' the ages one increasing purpose runs,
And the thoughts of men are widen'd with the process of the suns.

Yet, after 1859, the poets realized that Darwin's explanation was a naturalistic one that seemingly left no place for purpose, God, or spirit. A reaction against their earlier enthusiasm set in, a reaction intensified by the activities of the so-called social Darwinists, who justified the evils of nineteenth-century industrialism on the grounds that they wiped out the unfit and thus improved the race. So strong was Tennyson's own revulsion to such doctrines that in 1886 he wrote a counterblast to "Locksley Hall" called "Locksley Hall Sixty Years After":

Is there evil but on earth? or pain in every peopled sphere?
Well be grateful for the sounding watchword 'Evolution' here.

. . .
Is it well that while we range with Science, glorifying in the Time,
City children soak and blacken soul and sense in city slime?

. . .
There the smouldering fire of fever creeps across the rotted floor,
And the crowded coach of incest in the warrens of the poor.

Matthew Arnold considered that Darwinism had destroyed religion for thinking people. He rather regretted it, but felt that we had henceforth to face up to a world bare of the old consolation. "Dover Beach" is his most famous expression of this attitude. In it a lover speaks to his beloved as follows:

> Ah, love, let us be true
> To one another! for the world, which seems
> To lie before us like a land of dreams,
>   So various, so beautiful, so new,
>   Hath really neither joy, nor love, nor light,
> Nor certitude, nor peace, nor help for pain;
>   And we are here as on a darkling plain
>   Swept with confus'd alarms of struggle and flight,
>   Where ignorant armies clash by night.

In Algernon Charles Swinburne, however, the note of regret disappears. For him the extinction of the old beliefs by Darwinism promises weary man eternal rest.

> From too much love of living
> From hope and fear set free
> We thank with brief thanksgiving
>   Whatever gods may be
> That no life lives forever;
> That dead men rise up never;
> That even the weariest river
>   Winds somewhere safe to sea.

The evolution controversy was seized upon so avidly by popular novelists that for a while one could hardly tell whether one was reading a romance or an account of the Huxley-Wilberforce debates. Openly anti-Darwin were novels by such writers as Charles Reade, Catherine Lydell, Wilkie Collins, and Marie Corelli. In a typical anti-Darwin novel, the hero was a young clergyman (Church of England, of course) and the villain an agnostic scientist. The superior reasoning power of the clergyman converted the young scientist, who was then allowed to marry the heroine.

The other side of the debate was upheld by such novelists as George Gissing and Mrs. Humphrey Ward. In their novels, the formula was turned upside down. Now, the hero is an agnostic and the villain a sly, hypocritical clergyman. The most justly famous of such novels is Samuel Butler's *The Way of All Flesh*. In this novel all the good people are upstanding agnostics and the Christians are so inept that it is a wonder that they can offer enough opposition to keep the plot going.

The Way of All Flesh was of note in another way, too. Butler not only accepted Darwin but "improved" on him by introducing the Lamarckian concept of inherited memory. As might be expected, George Bernard Shaw followed Butler, not the later geneticists, in this matter.

Darwinism in the later nineteenth century fused with cosmic pessimism to help produce the naturalistic novel. One has only to read the novels of Thomas Hardy to see how Tennyson's "vision of the future" has changed.

It may be that the most long-lasting influence of Darwinism will be in the realm of science fiction. This genre hardly existed until the controversy over evolution popularized science as fictional material. H. G. Wells' novels *The War of the*

Worlds and *The Time Machine* were strictly Darwinian, and their modern imitators still show traces of their parentage.

Darwin cannot be credited (nor would he want to be) with all of this. Other forces were at work, too. Yet, unquestionably, nineteenth- and twentieth-century English literature would be far different without the movement linked with his name.

In Europe the impact was less great. French rationalism and German Biblical scholarship had long since destroyed the kind of complacency that England still possessed in Darwin's time. In America, on the other hand, the shock was as great as in England. However, most American literary men—in spite of all evidence to the contrary—remained determinedly optimistic.

BIBLIOGRAPHY

Barzun, Jacques. *Darwin, Marx, Wagner: Critique of a Heritage.* Boston, 1941.

Beech, J. W. *The Concept of Nature in Nineteenth-Century English Poetry.* New York, 1936.

Bergson, Henri. *L'Evolution créatrice.* Paris, 1948.

Bury, J. B. *The Idea of Progress: an Inquiry into its Origin and Growth.* London, 1920.

Bush, Douglas. *Science and English Poetry: a Historical Sketch, 1590–1950.* New York, 1950.

Henkin, L. J. *Darwinism in the English Novel, 1860–1910. The Impact of Evolution on Victorian Fiction.* New York, 1940.

Hofstadter, Richard. *Social Darwinism in American Thought.* Boston, 1955.

Hyman, S. E. *The Tangled Bank: Darwin, Marx, Frazer and Freud as Imaginative Writers.* New York, 1962.

Lovejoy, A. O. *The Great Chain of Being; a Study of the History of an Idea.* Cambridge, 1936.

Roppen, Georg. *Evolution and Poetic Belief. A Study in Some Victorian and Modern Writers.* Oslo, 1956.

Stevenson, Lionel. *Darwin Among the Poets.* Chicago, 1932.

Sears, P. B. *Charles Darwin: The Naturalist as a Cultural Force.* New York, 1950.

26 · Tolstoy (1828–1910)

THE MORAL OBJECTION to art, or at least some art, which Plato began and which was continued by censors in and out of the churches found its most persuasive spokesman in Leo Tolstoy. When he published *What is Art?* in 1898, he not only turned his back on most of modern art but even repudiated his own great novels. For this a modern lady novelist has called him the greatest betrayer since Judas. Yet Tolstoy himself felt that he was giving art a greater and truer importance than others were willing to grant it.

In the first pages of *What is Art?* Tolstoy expresses his shock at the immense sums of money and the enormous number of hours of labor spent for art, art which stunts human lives and transgresses against human love. Thousands upon thousands of people labor and pay taxes for the production of art from which they not only receive no benefit but which is usually harmful. How can the defenders of art justify its social cost? What, in other words, is art?

"Art is activity that produces beauty," says one aesthetician. Very well, says Tolstoy, but what then is beauty? If one turns to the writers on aesthetics, one finds nothing but confusion. Definitions of beauty there are, but usually in such confused language as to be incomprehensible. And, of course, one writer's definition is no sooner propounded than it is contradicted by the next writer's. Tolstoy decides that the very concept of beauty has only confused the matter, since whatever pleases the upper classes is said to have beauty. "In a word, that enjoyment is good because it is enjoyment." This is no definition but merely a shuffle to justify the art that actually exists. All definitions of art suffer from the fact that they are based on the assumption that pleasure is the end of art.

Then Tolstoy gives a definition that deliberately omits both "beauty" and "pleasure." "Art is a human activity consisting in this, that one man consciously by means of certain external signs, hands on to others feelings he has lived through, so that others are infected by these feelings and also experience them." A boy meets a wolf; he feels fear. In telling of his encounter, if he is able to infect the hearers with his feelings, he has created art. Or, if he invents such an encounter and recounts it so that his hearers experience his imagined emotions, this too is art.

How did the false idea that art is for pleasure's sake arise? It arose from the fact that men's estimation of the value of art depends on what they hold to be good and what evil. As long as people had a religious view of life they believed that art should propagate that view and should be accessible to everyone. At the Renaissance a great change came about. The upper classes, popes and bishops included, believed in nothing and could, then, have no other standard to judge art by than their personal preferences. Thus their own pleasure became the standard for good and bad art. The people were forgotten. Art became aristocratic and narrow in its appeal and has remained so. Indeed, the situation is so bad now that, says Tolstoy, the art which is most admired is that which is understood by no one. All of the falsities of modern art spring from the false organization of society. The fake art which predominates today is also an exclusive art and "can arise only on the slavery of the masses of the people, and can continue only as long as that slavery lasts. . . . Free the slaves of capital and it will be impossible to produce such refined art. To defend this art on the grounds that it gives pleasure to a few is as immoral as defending slavery because the master enjoys its comforts."

The restriction of art to the few, the "elect," is not only immoral but has resulted in a worsening, in a perversion, of art. True art demands the transmission of new, fresh feelings. However, the range of feelings experienced by the rich and powerful is much more limited than that of people who do the work of the world. What is the result? The art of the rich classes is limited to three insignificant feelings: pride, weariness of life, and, above all, sexual desire.

Side by side with its impoverished subject matter is the increasing obscurity of modern art. The greatest art is that which is intelligible to all men. When a Greek artist or Hebrew prophet composed, he composed for all. But now that art is for the few, the artist is content if his allusions are understood by his own little group. "It has come finally to this: that not only are haziness, mysteriousness, obscurity, and exclusiveness (shutting out the masses) elevated to the rank of a merit and condition of poetic art, but even inaccuracy, indefiniteness, and lack of eloquence, are held in esteem." In effect, says Tolstoy, some modern artists no longer even think of the little clan and write only for themselves. The theory that art must be difficult to be good is a heresy. The majority have always understood the very best art and still do, since art has nothing to do with learning. If art fails to move the majority of men, it proves not that they lack understanding, but that the art is bad.

Bad art is what reigns today. Indeed it cannot properly be called art at all. It is counterfeit art. There are four methods used to produce it. The first is to borrow the subjects and features from other works recognized to be "poetic." The second is to "imitate"; that is to say, to supply all sorts of details, the tone of voice of a character, minute description of his clothes, and the life. The third is to be "striking"; to use all sorts of sensational actions and effects, blending the beautiful and the hideous, the light and the dark. The fourth is to "interest"; to have an intricate plot, or to describe such interesting things as Egyptian or Roman life or the details of a mining operation. The reader will mistake interest for artistic impression. Now to be poetic, or realistic, or striking, or interesting is not to produce art.

The separation of the art of the upper classes from universal art has meant that the counterfeit has driven out the true. The conditions of modern society cooperate to produce the false. Artists have become professionals because they earn considerable sums of money by this activity. Obviously, to earn this money they must please the consumers of art, the town public.

Added to this is the growth of criticism. Art is now evaluated not by plain men but by perverted and self-confident critics. The critics prevert taste when they attempt to explain art. If the artist is successful in transmitting his feelings, there is nothing to explain. Being peculiarly unsusceptible to art, the critics cling to external criteria, particularly those of tradition and thus ruin the young artist by trying to make him conform.

Finally, schools of art spring up. Since no one can teach another how to feel, the schools can teach their students only how to contrive, to counterfeit. So, not only do they teach what is false, but they destroy in their pupils the capacity to produce real art. Real art depends first on feeling and secondly on perfection of form. Form is that which makes the feeling infectious, and thus art. Form cannot be taught. "Infection is only obtained when an artist finds those infinitely minute degrees of which a work of art consists, and only to the extent to which he finds them. And it is quite impossible to teach people by external means to find these minute degrees: they can only be found when a man yields to his feeling."

To what extent people have lost their capacity to appreciate true art is best shown by the esteem in which the operas of Wagner are held. All the methods by which art is counterfeited can be found in this German composer: borrowing, imitations, dramatic effects, and interest. His plot is a "stupid, incoherent fairy tale." His subjects are "poetic": a sleeping beauty, dwarfs, magic swords, etc. Moreover, all is imitated. Not only the decorations and the costumes but the very sounds. Wagner imitates the stroke of a hammer, the hissing of molten iron, and the singing of birds. His effects are deliberately striking: magic fires, scenes under water, darkness, and the like. And, of course, everything is interesting. Who will kill whom? Who is whose son? How will the rolling waves of the Rhine be expressed in music? And bravery? And apples?

So no wonder Wagner is a success. All the bad taste and false conceptions that make up counterfeit art reach their highest pitch of perfection in him. But Wagner is only an example, Tolstoy says. The proportion of real works of art to counterfeits is as one to some hundreds of thousands. Produced for people of false taste, they further corrupt that taste.

How amid the corruption of art can one recognize true art? For a country peasant of unperverted taste, this is easy. His natural instinct leads him to select the real work of art he needs. The educated (i.e., perverted) man has a much more difficult time.

The way to recognize good art is by its infectiousness. If on reading another man's work, there is immediately experienced a mental condition that unites you in a spiritual union with the author, you then know you are in the presence of true art. "A real work of art destroys in the consciousness of the recipient the separation between himself and the artist, and not that alone, but also between himself and all whose minds receive this work of art. In this freeing of our personality from its separation and isolation, in this uniting of it with others, lies the chief characteristic and the great attractive force of art." And, Tolstoy continues, "The stronger the infection the better is the art." The degree of infectiousness depends upon the sincerity of the author. He should be driven by an inner need to express his individual feeling, and he will search for the clearest expression for his feeling in order to transmit it successfully. Individuality, clarity, and sincerity are Tolstoy's touchstones.

Since Tolstoy has decided already that excellence of form renders a work of art infectious, the next question he must take up concerns the subject matter. "How," he asks "in the subject matter of art are we to decide what is good and what is bad?"

First, he says, we must recognize that art, like speech, is a means of communication and of progress. The evolution of knowledge takes place by new and better knowledge replacing the old; the evolution of the feelings proceeds by means of art. What feelings are considered most kind and most necessary for the well-being of mankind depend upon the religious perception of the age. (By religious perception Tolstoy does not mean what is taught by cults or churches.) Each age has a different perception. "The religious perception of our time in its widest and most practical application is the consciousness that our well-being, both material and spiritual, individual and collective, temporal and eternal, lies in the growth of brother-

hood among men—in their loving harmony with one another."
Exclusive art is bad art. Good art unites. There are two classes
of good art. The first is religious art, which transmits the feelings of love of God and one's neighbors (this, he reports, is
quite different from ecclesiastical art). The second is universal
art, which transmits the very simplest feelings, those which
are common to all men.

Among the examples of modern religious art which Tolstoy
gives are Schiller's *The Robbers*, Hugo's *Les Misérables*, Eliot's
Adam Bede, Stowe's *Uncle Tom's Cabin*, Dickens' *Tale of
Two Cities*, and Dostoevsky's works.

Among the works of the second class, he finds fewer worthy
of a place. *Don Quixote*, Molière's comedies, *David Copperfield*
and *The Pickwick Papers* by Dickens might be assigned to this
class but cannot be equated with such a universal story as the
Biblical one of Joseph and his brothers because each contains
a superfluity of details restricted to a certain time and a certain
locality. Of them all, however, Molière's plays are the most
universal. Of his own work, Tolstoy will admit "God Sees the
Truth, but Waits" into the category of religious art and "A
Prisoner in the Caucasus" into that of universal art. All of his
other productions he consigns to the category of bad art. Both
music and painting can express universal feelings too. Bad
painting and bad music (an example of the latter is Beethoven's
Ninth Symphony) are exclusive, not universal. Though Tolstoy
is convinced that his approach is the only correct one, he does
not attach much importance to the specific examples he gives.
"I belong," he says, "to the class of people whose taste has
been perverted by false training. And therefore, my old, inured
habits may cause me to err. . . ."

Again and again Tolstoy returns indignantly to what he considers the most shocking consequence of the absence of true art
in modern society, that is the enormous expenditure of labor,
the terrible exploitation of millions of people in order to produce a counterfeit art from which the people themselves gain
nothing. Most of modern art is for the upper classes. But even
they gain from it nothing but unhappiness and perverse attitudes toward life. The true enlightenment of the people has
been long held back by a false art which embodies church and

patriotic superstitions and disseminates vice as widely as possible.

Fortunately the cure lies at hand. A religious perception does exist in modern society. "However various in form their definitions of the destination of human life may be, all men in our times already admit that the highest well-being attainable by men is to be reached by their union with one another." This perception will guide the art of the future. This art will consist of a transmitting of the feelings which draw men together. No longer will the artists be selected from the upper classes or their hangers-on, but will be the gifted members of the whole people. Art will be accessible to all. Clearness, simplicity, and brevity will be demanded. The professional artist will no longer exist. "The art of the future will be produced by all members of the community who feel the need of such activity, but they will occupy themselves with art only when they feel such need."

Tolstoy admits the full consequences of his position. At the present if the question were asked whether it would be better to have no art than what is now considered art he would feel forced to stand with Plato. "I think that every reasonable and moral man would again decide the question as Plato decided it for his *Republic*, and as all the early Church-Christian, and Mohammedan teachers of mankind decided it, that is, would say, rather let there be no art at all than continue the depraving art or simulation of art, which now exists."

Yet Tolstoy, unlike Plato, believes in progress. He does not feel the question need be put or Plato's solution adopted. Men can learn to understand the error they are involved in and find a way to escape.

BIBLIOGRAPHY

Berlin, Isaiah. *The Hedgehog and the Fox; an Essay on Tolstoy's View of History*. New York, 1953.
Farrell, J. T. *Literature and Morality*. New York, 1947.
Gibian, George. *Tolstoy and Shakespeare*. The Hague, 1957.

Knight, G. W. *Shakespeare and Tolstoy*. London, 1934.

Maude, Aylmer. *Tolstoy on Art and Its Critics*. London, 1925.

Simmons, E. J. *Leo Tolstoy*. Boston, 1946; New York, 1960.

Steiner, George. *Tolstoy or Dostoevsky, an Essay in the Old Criticism*. New York, 1959.

Tolstoy, L. N. *Complete Works*; ed. by Leo Weiner. Boston, 1904–1905.

————. *What is Art? and Essays on Art*; tr. by Aylmer Maude. London, 1938.

27 · Marxism and Literature

THE WORLD-SHAKING economic and social theories of Karl Marx could not help but influence literary criticism. Marx insisted that literature, like every other cultural phenomenon, was a reflection of the basic economic structure of society. An epic, a poem, and a play are produced by the same forces that produce social classes and cannot be fully understood without reference to these forces. In his *Critique of Political Economy* he wrote:

Let us take for example, the relation of Greek art, and thereafter of Shakespeare, to their contemporaries. It is well known that Greek mythology constituted not only the arsenal of Greek art, but the very soil from which it grew. Is it possible that the attitude toward nature and social relationships, which lies at the basis of Greek fantasy, and therefore also of Greek art, could have existed in the presence of "self-acting mules," railways, locomotives, and the electric telegraph? What could Vulcan do against Roberts and Co., Jupiter against the lightning rod, and Hermes against the *Crédit Mobilier!* Every mythology overcomes, subjugates and forms the forces of nature in imagination and with the help of imagination. It disappears, consequently, with the actual mastery of these forces of nature.

Marx, unlike some of his more naïve followers, never held the crude conception that an advance in the economic sphere automatically produced a higher form of literature. On the contrary, he recognized that literary superstructures of extraordinary richness have developed in primitive economic systems. The Greek epic, for example, is not only not inferior to but is obviously superior to nineteenth-century novels which reflect a much more sophisticated economy.

Marx knew that cultural forms develop unevenly:

141

With reference to art, it is known that the fixed periods of its greatest development do not correspond with the general development of society, nor, consequently, with the development of the material basis of the latter, which constitutes, so to speak, the skeleton of its organization. For instance, compare the Greeks and also Shakespeare with their contemporaries.

With reference to the various forms of art, for example the epic, it is even acknowledged that they, in their classical form, constituting a period in world history, never could have been created, as soon as artistic production as such had begun; that, in this way, in the field of literature itself, these particular and highly significant forms, are possible only at a comparatively low stage of artistic development.

A real question was now raised, though. Since man's consciousness is a product of the society in which he lives, how can a person still obtain artistic pleasure from the *Iliad* or the *Odyssey*? Marx's answer to this question was extremely awkward:

A man cannot be transformed again into a child, or he becomes childish. But does he not take delight in a child's naïveté, and is not he himself obliged to strive toward this end, that he may produce his own true nature at a higher stage? In the nature of a child, in every era, does there not come to life again the character of this era, in its artless truth? And why should not the childhood of human society, there, where it has the most beautiful development of all, possess for us an external charm, as a stage which never repeats itself? There are uneducated children, and there are children who have the wisdom of old age. Many of the ancient peoples belong to this category. The Greeks were normal children. The fascination which their art possesses for us does not lie in its contradiction to that undeveloped stage of society, upon which it grew up. On the contrary, that art appears to be the result of that stage of society, and to be indissolubly linked with the fact that the immature social relations under which it arose, and under which alone it could arise, can never be repeated again.

Unsatisfactory as this was, it had the virtue of wedding Marxism to the humanistic tradition and of allowing Marx's literary followers to judge in terms of taste as well as of economics.

The rapid spread of Marxist politics throughout the world introduced Marx's literary theories to all countries. Marxism helped create a social perspective that influenced much literary scholarship. In America, particularly during the years of the great depression, such notable critics as Edmund Wilson, Newton Arvin, and F. O. Matthiessen made intelligent use of Marx's methods to enrich America's knowledge of her cultural heritage.

Granville Hicks ambitiously attempted to fit the history of American literature into a Marxist framework in *The Great Tradition* (1933). His apparent success was made possible by the rather naïve assumption that all writers who found something to criticize in American society were spiritual kin to the American Communists and their literary fellow travelers. Those American writers content with "blind estheticism" were dismissed as being unworthy of the "great tradition."

Unlike Karl Marx, the American sympathizers with Marxism did not hesitate to make identification between esthetics and politics. Hicks could write, "As we have seen, industrialism became more and more important in American life, the implication of capitalism grew clearer and clearer, the lines of the class struggle were drawn more and more sharply, and consequently the cost of evasion greater and greater. Comparing Edith Wharton with Sara Orne Jewett, or Robert Frost with Emily Dickinson, we have realized that it has become increasingly difficult for those who ignore industrialism to create a vital literature."

When he evaluated the position of the writers of his period he found that "the central fact in American life is the class struggle" and that the writer who allies himself with the proletariat will be able to write better since he will see clearly the underlying forces which shape society, since he will not be practicing the self-deception of the art-for-art's-sake writers.

Yet, in spite of its exaggeration of the Marxist literary theory, *The Great Tradition* had the virtue of never forgetting that literature, though shaped by social forces, is not identical with them. This saving grace was sadly lacking in other Marxist critics. For instance, the avowed Communist Joseph Freeman, in his introduction to an anthology, *Proletarian Literature in The United States* (1935), had no interest in literature per se. For him a poem or novel could be evaluated only in political terms: Did it or did it not advance the revolution? He wrote:

Whatever role it may have played in epochs preceding ours, whatever may be its function in the classless society of the future, social war today has made it the subject of partisan polemic. The form of polemic varies with the social class for which the critic speaks, as well as with his personal intelligence, integrity, and courage. The Communist says frankly: art, an instrument in the class struggle, must be developed by the proletariat as one of its weapons. The fascist, with equal frankness, says: art must serve the aims of the capitalist state. The liberal, speaking for the middle class which vacillates between monopoly capital and the proletariat, between fascism and communism, poses as the "impartial" arbiter in this, as in all other social disputes. He alone presumes to speak from above the battle, in the "scientific" spirit.

By implication Freeman even rejects Marx's theory that the classics appeal to something basic in our makeup by questioning whether any human experience can be considered changeless or universal. People of different historical times have different experiences, and even within the same historical period the experience, and thus the human nature, of men of different classes is different. Indeed, Freeman identifies literature with the content of literature in much the same way as Plato did:

The class basis of art is most obvious when a poem, play, or novel deals with a political theme. Readers and critics then react to literature, as they do in life, in an unequivocal manner. There is a general assumption, however, that certain "biologic" experiences transcend class factors. Love, anger, hatred, fear, the desire to please, to pose, to mystify, even vanity and self-love, may be universal motives; but the form they take, and above all the factors which arouse them, are conditioned, even determined, by class culture. Consider Proust's superb study of a dying aristocracy and a bourgeoisie in full bloom; note the things which arouse pride, envy, shame in a Charlus or a Madame Verdurin. Can anyone in his senses say that these things— an invitation to a party at a duke's home, a long historical family tree—would stir a worker to the boastful eloquence of a Guermantes or a Verdurin? Charlus might be angry at Charlie Morel for deceiving him with a midinette; could the Baron conceive what it is to be angry with a foreman for being fired?

The identification of literature with its political and ethical content led even Plato, it may be remembered, to take the ultimate step of suggesting that not only should the magistrate prescribe the content of literature but should decide who was and who was not allowed to write. In Soviet Russia, particularly during the black years of Stalin, Plato's suggestions were followed to the letter. The party line on literature came from the Kremlin, and every pressure was exerted on poets and novelists to see that they wrote what was wanted. The party hacks often discovered that by the time their compositions were in print the party line had changed and that what they had written was "objectively counter-revolutionary." The Kremlin by its use of police terror decided in the most dramatic fashion who should not write, often by the device of a shot in the back of the head. Since the state controlled the printing and distribution of all books, a complete system of rewards and punishments was at hand to decide who should be considered a writer and who should not.

Under such a system literary criticism reached its nadir. A review of a new book in 1951 in *Pravda* contained these sentences: "It is a pity that not a single modern Soviet writer is represented in the pages of this anthology by a novelette, short story, or pamphlet exposing the beastlike essence of American imperialism." *Izvestia* in the same year critized a book of poems as having too much "beauty" and not an iota of praise for Soviet industries. "Only once," the paper continues, "did the poet notice a girl construction worker."

That Karl Marx could not have envisioned the extremes to which the Soviet totalitarians would put his literary theories is obvious. We know, for instance, that his colleague Frederick Engels wrote the following in a letter to an early "proletarian" novelist who asked for Engel's help in popularizing his novel: "Look at your heroine, with her dialectical materialist eyes and her economic determinist nose and her surplus value mouth. *You* take her in your arms and *you* kiss her. I know I wouldn't want to."

BIBLIOGRAPHY

Burgum, E. B. *The Novel and the World's Dilemma*. New York, 1947.
Farrell, James T. *A Note on Literary Criticism*. New York, 1936.
Hicks, Granville. *The Great Tradition: an Interpretation of American Literature Since the Civil War*. New York, 1933.

Howe, Irving, and Lewis Coster (with the assistance of Julius Jacobson). *The American Communist Party: A Critical History*. Boston, 1957.

Klingender, F. D. *Marxism and Modern Art*. London, 1943.

Lipshitz, Mikhail. *The Philosophy of Art of Karl Marx*. New York, 1938.

Matthiessen, F. O. *American Renaissance: Art and Expression in the Age of Emerson and Whitman*. New York, 1941.

Plekhanov, Georgi. *Art and Society*; tr. from the Russian; Critics' Group series. New York, 1936.

Proletarian Literature in The United States; ed. by G. Hicks, M. Gold, and others. New York, 1935.

Sokolov, Y. M. *Russian Folklore*; tr. by C. R. Smith. New York, 1950

Trotsky, Leon. *Literature and Revolution*. New York, 1925.

28 · Bergson (1859-1941)

THOUGH PRIMARILY a professional philosopher, Henri Bergson had a considerable influence on literature. He presented a doctrine which seemed to offer an escape from the materialistic determinism of the Darwinian school, one which gave the poet and the artist a position superior to that of the man of science. Zola had felt that he was doing well when he offered to the novelist the possibility of being as "realistic" as the scientist. Bergson enunciates a philosophy which claims that it is the artist, not the scientist, who penetrates to reality.

The scientist attempts to arrive at knowledge by analysis, that is to say, he anatomizes and mechanically arranges experiences. In so doing he is false to the continuous, dynamic, free flow of life. The scientist is artificial. For, as Bergson sees it, life is a "continuous process indefinitely pursued, an indivisible process, on which each visible organism rides during the short interval of time given it to live."

True reality is the *élan vital*, the vital impulse that creates, that makes for continuous evolution. Matter is that which it struggles against. The *élan vital* strives toward creativity and individuality against matter, which would drag it down to inertness, to death. It is the artist who by his *intuition* is able to penetrate through matter to reality.

In *Laughter: An Essay on the Meaning of the Comic* (1900), Bergson shows how his philosophy may be of use in literary criticism. "What," he asks, "is the object of art?" It is to get at reality by brushing aside the veil that keeps us from entering into immediate communion with things and ourselves. This veil

147

we weave ourselves. We have to live, and "life demands that we grasp things in their relations to our own needs." In order to live, to act, to respond appropriately, we accept the utilitarian side of things. In other words, we deliberately simplify reality for practical reasons. We wipe out the differences between things in order to emphasize useful similarities. That is to say, we classify. "The *individuality* of things or of beings escapes us, unless it is materially to our advantage to perceive it. Even when we do take note of it—as when we distinguish one man from another—it is not the individuality itself that the eye grasps, i.e., an entirely original harmony of forms and colors, but only one or two features that will make practical recognition easier." Most words denote classes, kinds of things, and they screen us from the individual thing. Even our own individuality escapes us.

But from time to time nature raises up souls that are more detached from life. If a soul were completely detached from action, it would be the soul of an artist such as has never been seen, since all forms, colors, and sounds of the physical world would be perceived by it in its native purity. But nature is not this generous. Instead, she usually allows the artist to lift the veil in one direction only. This direction corresponds to what is called a sense. This is the reason for the diversity of the arts.

If the artist sees "the inner life of things . . . appearing through their forms and colors," he is called a painter. He is able to reveal nature to us by diverting us from "the prejudices of form and color that come between ourselves and reality." If the artist is able to attain to the emotion, the original mood, which lies beneath the commonplace, conventional expression that conceals the individual mental state, he is a poet. By animating words with a life of their own, the poet suggests to us things that speech is not calculated to express. If the artist penetrates still deeper and grasps certain rhythms of life which cannot even roughly be translated into language, he is a musician.

"So art, whether it be painting or sculpture, poetry or music, has no other object than to brush aside the utilitarian symbols, the conventional and socially accepted generalities, in short, everything that veils reality from us, in order to bring us face to face with reality itself." This direct vision of reality implies an immateriality, a disinterestedness, that may truly be called idealism. Thus, contradictory as it may sound, Bergson suggests that "it is only through ideality that we can resume contact with reality."

Having laid down this law of art, Bergson proceeds to illustrate it by discussing dramatic art. Like the other arts, dramatic art brings to light the reality which our interests and necessities conceal from us. "Poetry always expresses inward states." The most violent of these inward states are those that arise from contact with our fellowmen. Strong attraction and repulsion take place whenever people are brought together. Yet, since man must live in society, he must learn the conventions which enable him to conceal the inner fire of his passions.

Drama provides us with pleasure by stirring up that which lies beneath "the quiet humdrum life that reason and society have fashioned for us." What interests us when we see or read a drama is not so much what we have been told about others as the glimpse we catch of ourselves. An appeal is made to memories rooted deep within us. "So it is indeed a deeper reality that drama draws up from beneath our superficial and utilitarian attainments. . . ."

The art of the drama, like all art, aims at what is individual. Nothing could be more individual than the character of Hamlet. He is universally true only in the sense that he is universally accepted and regarded as a living character. It is the sincerity of the artist which makes his unique product convincing. So, dealing as it does with the individual, tragedy is genuine art.

Comedy, on the other hand, is not genuine art, says Bergson, since it concerns itself not with individuals but with the classes. We can say, "a Tartuffe," but we could never say, "a Lear." For whereas the tragic hero is a unique individual, the comic character represents a general trait.

The tragic poet, does not, it then seems, need to study other men. Shakespeare was not Macbeth or Hamlet or Othello, but he might have been if the circumstances were such and so and the poet's will consented. Nothing living can result from merely recomposing life. "Poetic imagination is but a fuller view of reality. If the characters created by a poet give us the impres-

sion of life, it is only because they are the poet himself . . .
the poet plumbing the depths of his own nature in so powerful
an effort of inner observation, that he lays hold of the potential
in the real, and takes up what nature has left as a mere outline
and sketch in his soul in order to make of it a finished work of
art."

The comic poet proceeds in an exactly opposite way. He observes others and attempts to express the average. In other
words, like the scientist, he abstracts and generalizes. His purpose is to raise laughter in order to correct. The more he generalizes, the more persons he reaches.

Having put forth the thesis that art is individual, Bergson is
compelled to deny that comedy is genuine art. True, it belongs
to art insofar as its only visible aim is to please, but being general it contrasts with other works of art. So, he concludes, "comedy lies midway between art and life. It is not disinterested as
genuine art is. By organizing laughter, comedy accepts social
life as a natural environment; it even obeys an impulse of social
life. And in this respect it turns its back upon art which is a
breaking away from society and a return to pure nature."

At least Bergson is consistent. So far away is he from the
social point of view of earlier periods that he turns the classical
doctrine upside down. The classical critics said that one imitated the individual in order to attain to an ideal which, because it is ideal, is general. The poet was urged to imitate individual heroes, say, in order to attain to the ideal of the Hero.
Bergson's idealism teaches the opposite. The true work of art is
never general; it is always individual.

BIBLIOGRAPHY

Adolphe. Lydie. *L'Univers bergsonien*. Paris, 1955.
Arbour, Roméo. *Henri Bergson et les lettres françaises*. Paris,
    1955.
Bergson, Henri. *Creative Evolution*; tr. by Arthur Mitchell. Lon-
    don, 1911.

————. *Laughter; an Essay on the Meaning of the Comic*; tr. by Cloudseley Brereton and Fred Rothwell. London, 1911.

————. *L'Evolution créatrice*. 5th ed., Paris, 1909.

————. *Le Rire; Essai sur la signification du comique*. 5th ed. Paris, 1908.

Hanna, Thomas. *The Bergsonian Heritage*. New York, 1962.

Lovejoy, A. O. *Bergson and Romantic Evolutionism*. Berkeley, 1914.

Mathewson, Louise. *Bergson's Theory of the Comic in the Light of English Comedy*. University of Nebraska, 1920.

Szathmary, A. *The Aesthetic Theory of Bergson*. Cambridge, 1937.

29 · Croce (1866–1952)

BENEDETTO CROCE is one of the most influential of modern critics. His followers rank him as the leading exponent of the science of aesthetics. In the history of critical thought Croce is particularly interesting because he is the one who most intelligently protests against the extreme individualism of the impressionists and the positivistic, naturalistic, and materialistic approaches of many of the nineteenth-century critics.

The clearest summary of his ideas is to be found in the article "Aesthetics," which he wrote for the fourteenth edition of the *Encyclopædia Britannica*. In this, Croce attempts to distinguish art from other forms of activity with which it has been confused. Art is not philosophy because philosophy is "logical thinking of the universal categories of being." Art is not history because history must employ the critical distinction between reality and nonreality. Art is not natural science because natural science depends upon the classification of historical fact and is thus made abstract; nor is it mathematical science because mathematics operates with abstractions. Art is not the play of fancy because fancy merely searches to amuse itself with likenesses. Art is not feeling in its immediacy since the poet does not totter under the emotions he sings. Art is not instruction or oratory since art is not limited by any practical ends. And, finally, art cannot be confused with any other forms directed to the production of certain effects whether these be pleasure, utility, or righteousness.

What, then, is art? It is lyrical or pure intuition and is the first form of knowledge. It is distinguished from the second form of knowledge, which is logic. Note that Croce does not say that intuition is a step in the production of art. It *is* art. When the artist has created a form in all its completeness in his mind the proper activity of art has ceased. Art is always a form of self-expression and is always internal.

In other words, before the painting is painted, the statue carved, or the poem written, the aesthetic work has already taken place. Art is an ideal activity. To be sure, the artist may then paint his picture, or carve his statue, or write his poem, but this is not necessary. This latter act is merely an externalization that produces a practical fact or a fact of will, but one which is quite separate from art.

Assuming that the sculptor wills to leave durable traces by carving a statue, the statue itself is not a work of art. It is merely a physical stimulant which may induce an intuition in the beholder. The material in itself has no importance. The practicing artist who speaks of the form of his work being molded by his material is speaking in terms exactly opposite to Croce's.

At first glance it would seem that, since the intuition of the artist is unique, the critic is not needed. Yet in his *Poetry* Croce insists that the work of the critic is necessary work and takes it upon himself to show him how to judge and how not to judge.

"The judgment of poetry," he says, "has a single indivisible category, that of beauty." Strictly speaking, there can be no distinction or division of the beautiful. But since the ugly is a lack of aesthetic coherence, it is possible to specify the incoherence. Thus we have many terms for forms of ugliness, but beauty is beauty. In reading these remarks of Croce, one is reminded of the first sentence of Tolstoy's *Anna Karenina*: "Happy families are all alike; every unhappy family is unhappy in its own way."

Thus, continues Croce, the old distinctions are nothing but abstractions. To speak of the sublime, the tragic, the comic, and the like is merely to be empirical. The same is true of the division of poetry into lyric, epic, and dramatic. Even if the duality is reduced to lyric and drama, nothing is found except the relation of matter to poetic expression, of sentiment to intuition. The famous division between classical and romantic poetry is open to the same objections from Croce's point of view. Here again the sole division that he will allow to be considered is that between the beautiful and the ugly.

Since poetry is poetry, all conventional divisions are pseudo-aesthetic and misleading. They are no less so when they embody political and social concepts. Poetry of the classical type has been identified with the Roman and neo-Latin peoples, romantic poetry with the Germanic peoples. Some even speak of peculiarly Germanic poetry, which can be written and judged only by Germans. Others speak of class poetry and talk of proletarian poetry, bourgeois poetry, and the like. To all such divisions Croce opposes the indivisibility of complete and true poetry. Poetry is poetry.

What should the critic concern himself with since the old categories are superficial? What is his function? He cannot merely spend his time with the abstract relation of concepts or content himself with giving a logical equivalent for the poem. If logic were enough, poetry would not exist. He must attach himself to the individual reality of the poem. His function is to give a characterization of the poem, that is, to determine its content or that which is its moving force. Then he may assign what has been determined to the psychological class best suited to it. But even if he places the poem in a satisfactory class, he is merely working in terms of general concepts, and since poetry is individual, the critic's formula can never coincide with the poem. There is always an abyss between the two.

Why then bother with criticism? Croce's answer is that the critic does the necessary spadework. By his historical research, his taste, and his trained imagination, he teaches others where to begin so that they will not make false starts. This is a beneficial activity, even though the critic is unable to make men perceive and enjoy poetry. This is something that they must do for themselves.

If we do not feel that this is completely satisfactory, we can at least see why Croce could not make it more so. Starting as he does with his argument that poetry begins and ends in itself, that the work of art exists in the mind of the artist, that the "materialization" of the work is merely a matter of will, he cannot without being false to himself allow the critic to explain what must remain unexplainable.

Indeed, Croce seems to say that if we want to judge Dante we must become Dante. How else can we obtain to Dante's individual intuition which is, he reminds us, unique?

BIBLIOGRAPHY

Croce, Benedetto. *Aesthetics as Science of Expression and General Linguistic*; tr. by Douglas Ainslie. 2nd ed. London, 1922.
————. "Aesthetics"; tr. by R. G. Collingwood. *Encyclopædia Britannica*, 14th edition. New York, 1929.
————. *The Defence of Poetry*; tr. by E. F. Carritt. Oxford, 1933.
————. *La Poesia*. Bari, 1937.
Orsini, Gian N. *Benedetto Croce, Philosopher of Art and Literary Critic*. Carbondale, Ill., 1961.
Spingarn, J. E. *The New Criticism*. New York, 1911.

30 · Freudianism and Literature

SINCE THE GREATEST writers have also been among many other things intuitive psychologists, the theories of psychoanalysis seemed particularly suited for the better understanding of literature. Indeed, Sigmund Freud often spoke as if his contribution were merely to give experimental evidence to what the poets and philosophers had long since revealed. He praised them as being among "the few to whom it is vouchsafed . . . with hardly any effort to salvage from the whirlpool of their emotions the deepest truth to which we others have to force our way, ceaselessly groping among torturing uncertainties." (*Civilization and Its Discontents*, 1930) The insights of Dostoevsky, for instance, anticipated so many of Freud's that one could almost construct Freudian theories from this one novelist alone.

Freud theorized that the writer was a man who satisfied erotic drives which could not be satisfied in real life by creating a fantasy life where he could obtain instinctual satisfaction in a sublimated form. If this implied that the writer was a neurotic, it also implied that literary creation was a form of therapy which enabled the writer to control his instinctual drives better than the vast number of neurotics who were not artists.

To phrase it another way, writers seem to have fewer inhibitions than the rest of men. For example: Freud discovered in Stendhal's *Henri Brulard* (Chap. III) the following amazing passage: "In loving [my mother], I had exactly the same character as when later I loved Alberthe de Rubempré with real passion . . . since then my way of seeking happiness has changed little, with the single exception that in what constitutes the physical side of love I was then what Caesar would be, if he came back to earth with regard to the use of cannon and small arms. I should soon have learned, and it would have changed nothing in my tactics. I wanted to cover my Mother with kisses, and for her to have no clothes on. She loved me passionately and kissed me often. I returned her kisses, with such ardor that she was sometimes obliged to run away. I abhorred my father when he came to interrupt our kisses. I always wanted to kiss her bosom."

Seldom did a writer so clearly recognize his major desires to kill his father and to make love to his mother. Usually the material from his unconscious was subject to certain distortions which allowed it to be accepted by his conscious mind. The most famous example of this is the *Oedipus Rex* of Sophocles, so famous that Freud borrowed the name of Sophocles' king for the fundamental complex of all men. In the Oedipus legend, the hero kills his father and sleeps with his mother but does this in ignorance of their true identities. This, said Freud, was a poetic presentation of the fact that the adult is no longer conscious of his Oedipal experience. In the same fashion the prediction of the oracle that Oedipus will do what he does symbolized the inevitability of the fate which requires us all to live through this experience. Even the self-blinding of Oedipus can be considered as a poetic form of self-castration.

Since every work of literature cannot but reflect, in however distorted a form, the author's own reaction to the Oedipal situation, Freudians could claim that they had an answer to the age-old question of why literature moves us. It does so, they said, by presenting in symbolic form our own most fundamental desires. In a sense, then, the reader relives his own most important experience by the aid of poetic symbols.

Though this theory explained the value of literature per se, it raised another question. Since all literary works deal with the Oedipal situation, why are not all literary works equally satisfactory? To answer this, Freud, like critics of other schools, fell back on the concept of genius which was as unexplainable to him as to anyone else. "Before the problem of the creative artist, analysis must lay down its arms." ("Dostoevsky and Parricide") Yet, Freud seemed to imply that works of literature whose symbols most clearly reflect the universal Oedipal experience are the best. What the two dramas considered the greatest in our heritage, Sophocles' *Oedipus Rex* and Shakespeare's *Hamlet*, have in common is that both present the unconscious drives of all of us with a minimum of distortion.

Freud's English follower Ernest Jones examined these plays in his book *Hamlet and Oedipus* (1949). Shakespeare's plot is a variation of the *Oedipus Rex* plot. Hamlet's father has been killed by his uncle Claudius, who has married Hamlet's mother Gertrude. Hamlet's attitudes toward the two crimes, the murder of the father and the incest of the mother, differ profoundly. He hates the first crime and recognizes his duty to avenge it, but it does not fill him with the absolute disgust that his mother's incestuous relations with Claudius do. Even before he learns that his father has been murdered, his depression at the idea of his mother and Claudius as man and wife makes him contemplate suicide.

> O that this too too solid flesh would melt,
> Thaw, and resolve itself into a dew!
> Or that the Everlasting had not fix'd
> His canon 'gainst self-slaughter! O God! God!
> How weary, stale, flat, and unprofitable
> Seem to me all the uses of this world!
> Fie on't! ah, fie! 'Tis an unweeded garden
> That grows to seed; things rank and gross in nature
> Possess it merely. That it should come to this!
> But two months dead! Nay, not so much, not two.
> So excellent a king, that was to this
> Hyperion to a satyr; so loving to my mother
> That he might not beteem the winds of heaven
> Visit her face too roughly. Heaven and earth!
> Must I remember? Why, she would hang on him
> As if increase of appetite had grown
> By what it fed on; and yet, within a month—
> Let me not think on't! Frailty, thy name is woman!—
> A little month, or ere those shoes were old
> With which she followed my poor father's body
> Like Niobe, all tears—why she, even she
> (O God! a beast that wants discourse of reason
> Would have mourn'd longer) married with my uncle;
> My father's brother, but no more like my father
> Than I to Hercules. Within a month,
> Ere yet the salt of most unrighteous tears

> Had left the flushing in her galled eyes,
> She married. O, most wicked speed, to post
> With such dexterity to incestuous sheets!
> It is not, nor it cannot come to good.
> But break my heart, for I must hold my tongue!

Even when he becomes convinced that Claudius is the murderer of old Hamlet, he cannot bring himself to kill him. Unlike the traditional hero of the revenge tragedy, he seems almost to search for excuses to delay his vengeance. When a perfect opportunity is offered him to kill Claudius, he finds he cannot do it and rationalizes his inability by pretending that if he slew Claudius, who was on his knees presumably praying, he would send his soul straight to heaven.

The key to all this, continues Jones, lies in the fact that Hamlet unconsciously identifies himself with Claudius. For has not Claudius enacted in life the deepest desires of Hamlet? Has he not killed the father and made love to the mother? Thus to kill Claudius would be the psychic equivalent of committing suicide. Hamlet's mind continually plays with two ideas: killing his uncle and killing himself. It is not until the end of the play, when the poison is already in Hamlet's veins, that he can raise his hand against Claudius, his surrogate self.

Nor do Hamlet's other actions fail to fit into this fundamental pattern. His treatment of Ophelia springs, at least in part, from his desire to use her as a way of making his mother jealous, particularly in the rather coarse scene where he refuses to sit by his mother and throws himself at Ophelia's feet with the remark, "No, good mother, here's metal more attractive." With no hesitation he can run his sword through Ophelia's father Polonius, since Polonius is a mere father image and not like Claudius the son too.

Regardless of the merit or lack of merit of this interpretation, it should at least be understood before it is attacked. Several critics have dismissed it as utter nonsense by declaring that since Prince Hamlet is merely words on paper, not a living being, he cannot have an Oedipus complex. This is beside the point. Freud and Jones were not complete idiots. The Oedipus complex which is revealed in the play is not that of the characters but of a man of flesh and blood, William Shakespeare.

The most valid objection to Freudian criticism from a literary standpoint is that it tends to "type" the characters in a play or novel much in the same way as the old genre criticism did. Since the Freudian stereotypes are, of necessity, generalizations about human nature, the individuality of the hero of a play or novel is overlooked. What Jones tells us about Hamlet as an Oedipal type, even if true, does not in the last analysis tell us why this individual character has so much more meaning for us than innumerable other Oedipal types in literature.

As might be imagined, the various schools of psychoanalysis that come after Freud have, in changing his doctrines, changed psychoanalytic literary criticism. For example the followers of Adler substituted the inferiority and superiority complexes as the key to literary character analysis. Those who held to the teachings of Jung preferred to emphasize the collective unconscious of the race as revealed in the character, an unconscious which contained mystic elements. The tendency in more recent psychoanalytical criticism is to borrow concepts from all these schools, an eclecticism that parallels the eclecticism of many practicing psychoanalysts.

Perhaps the most extreme form of psychoanalytical criticism has been based on the ideas of Dr. Edmund Bergler, a former director of the Vienna Psychoanalytic Clinic. From his analyses of thirty-six practicing writers, he came to the conclusion that Freud was wrong in thinking that creative artists express their repressed desires in disguised form. On the contrary, Bergler contended, the writer expressed defenses against his breast complex. The infant has a masochistic attachment to the mother since, when the breast is refused him, he takes both pleasure and pain from this refusal. Writing is, then, "a self-creative alibi sickness," since the writer unconsciously identifies words and milk. As he pours out the words on paper he is saying, "See, even if you, mother, do not give milk, I do." In this manner he denies his dependency on the mother.

In a study of the English romantics called *The Demon Lover* (1949), Arthur Wormhoudt applied Bergler's findings to the poetry of Wordsworth, Coleridge, Keats, Shelley, and Byron. Wormhoudt claimed that the poetry of these men show that all five had this breast complex. In a discussion of the poetic symbols they used, he went so far as to say:

Domes, mountains, pyramids, and cups by their mere shape are suggestive of the breast. Streams, fountains, and floods can be used to symbolize it as the source of liquid nourishment, just as apples and food in general may also be associated with the same aspect. A more complicated symbol for the child at the breast is the tree which, insofar as it sucks liquid from mother earth in the spring, breathes through its leaves all summer long, and is drained of its sap in the fall, has definite oral connotations. Birds, however, seem to be the most frequent symbols for the breast in Romantic literature and this at first seems difficult to understand, especially in view of the fact that flying has some associations with sexual intercourse and that bird and penis are sometimes identified. Nevertheless, compared to most animals, birds are not easy to distinguish sexually —differences in color being negligible for the child in this respect. This makes them good symbols for the presexual emotions of the breast complex. They also come and go with inexplicable suddenness and this may symbolize the fact that the child had no control over comings and goings of the breast. Especially important for poets is the fact that birds are among the few species of animals which express their emotions in compulsive song—a valuable detail in the unconscious symbolization of the identification words-milk.

Here, in a rather extreme form, is evident the tendency of psychoanalytic criticism to fall into the listing of types and to generalize so broadly that the individual quality of the poem disappears from sight. Yet, Freudian insights, intelligently applied, give hope that critics may once again find ways of talking about literature in a genuinely comparative manner.

BIBLIOGRAPHY

Barber, C. L. *Shakespeare's Festive Comedy*. Princeton, 1959.
Basler, R. P. *Sex, Symbolism, and Psychology in Literature*. New Brunswick, 1948.
Bergler, Edmund. *The Writer and Psychoanalysis*. New York, 1950.
Freud, Sigmund. *Leonardo da Vinci: a Psychosexual Study of*

an Infantile Reminiscence; tr. by A. A. Brill. New York, 1910.

———. *Moses and Monotheism;* tr. by Katherine Jones. London, 1939.

———. *An Outline of Psychoanalysis;* tr. by James Strachey. New York, 1949.

———. *Wit and its Relation to the Unconscious;* tr. by A. A. Brill. New York, 1916.

Hoffman, F. J. *Freudianism and the Literary Mind.* Baton Rouge, 1957.

Jones, Ernest. *Hamlet and Oedipus.* New York, 1949.

Neider, Charles. *The Frozen Sea: a Study of Franz Kafka.* New York, 1948.

Obendorf, Clarence. *The Psychiatric Novels of O. W. Holmes.* New York, 1943.

Rank, Otto. *Art and Artist: Creative Urge and Personality Development.* New York, 1932.

Wormhoudt, Arthur. *The Demon Lover: a Psychoanalytical Approach to Literature.* New York, 1949.

31 · I. A. Richards (1893–   )

WITH FEWER and fewer thinkers accepting the old values, the question arose if it were proper even to ask whether art had value. Yet the consequences of the refusal to ask this question worried many. It meant declining to consider what most past critics had believed was the fundamental problem of literary criticism. But if, like Tolstoy, one could not feel that a Christian morality made clear what was "good" and what was "bad," how could one approach the problem of value?

I. A. Richards, in his *Principles of Literary Criticism* (rev. ed. 1934), comes to the conclusion that it is possible on the basis of modern knowledge to construct a psychological theory of value that will enable us to compare the worth of experiences, literary or otherwise. He observes that no one with a knowledge of the data supplied by anthropology could think that peoples of different habits, races, and civilizations hold to the same conceptions of good. Certain peoples look upon the public consumption of food as highly indecent; others consider forgiveness of one's enemies to be immoral.

Nor are the findings of the psychologists less significant. The value judgments of infants have struck dismay into the conventional moralists. The concept of the *infans polypervers* can give no comfort to those who think that the morality of Christianity or any other religion is innate. How then is the primitive, newborn animal transformed into, say, a bishop? By such social pressures as custom, public opinion, beliefs, and examples, his impulses and desires are at each stage of his development metamorphosed into a new form, or what

Richards calls a degree of systematization. Yet this systematization can never be complete. Impulses of a contradictory nature always exist. Some of them are psychologically incompatible. For instance, there are people who cannot smoke and write at the same time. There are also the indirect incompatibilities which arise as the consequences of one's acts.

To conduct our life, we must organize our impulses so that the most important of them obtain success. Here is the problem of value. How can we distinguish between organizations of impulses? Which yield the greater or lesser value?

To answer this question, Richards divides impulses into "appetencies" and "aversions." An appetency is a seeking after, an aversion is a withdrawing from. That which satisfies an appetency is valuable. Apart from consequences, anyone will prefer to satisfy a greater rather than a lesser number of equal appetencies. The only psychological reason for not satisfying a desire is that the consequences will be the frustration of more important desires. Morality is thus a question of expediency.

But what is "important" is not yet defined. Certain needs must be satisfied before others are even possible. Eating, drinking, sleeping, and breathing must be carried on as a condition for less primitive activities. Second in importance to these needs are those which enable man, a social creature, to communicate and cooperate. Thus we may consider that there is a hierarchy of values.

In a civilized society, certain activities originally valuable as means become of such importance through their connection with other activities that without them life is thought to be intolerable. Men prefer death rather than to be cut off from normal relations with their fellow beings. Even the conscientious objector and the martyr are not exceptions to this rule. They are so organized that it is only by acting as they do that they can satisfy their dominant impulses.

Now, since the importance of an impulse can be defined as "the extent of the disturbance of other impulses in the individual's activities which the thwarting of the impulse involves," it is possible to examine the relative merits of different systematizations. Every systematization sacrifices certain impulses, but in some the price paid is greater than in others.

The one which is least wasteful of human possibilities is the best. From this point of view valuation is possible. Both the repressed victim of conscience and the debauchee may be considered as paying excessive prices for the organization they achieve.

Obviously society can and does require the individuals who compose it to organize their impulses in a way consistent with the interests of society as a whole, but the organization of an individual may be better as well as worse than the standard of the group. Any stable system demands an element of sacrifice. This explains the tenacity with which custom is clung to and the intolerance which is directed against the new. Socrates is dealt with as severely as a murderer. The façade of public morality is buttressed with such contrivances as the wills of the gods, taboos, immediate intuitions, public opinion, and the like. Any stable system is better than no system for the organization of public behavior, but all hitherto existing social organizations have demanded an appalling amount of sacrifice.

Customs change, to be sure, but the real danger arises from the fact that they change more slowly than conditions. The obsolete virtues (such as nationalism armed with weapons of great destruction, or the glorification of fecundity in conditions of overpopulation) involve a growing danger. Unless a more adaptable morality is devised, we may be overwhelmed within a generation.

How do we as individuals and how does society through us achieve better organization? Chiefly, says Richards, through the influence of other minds. It is primarily through literature and the arts that these influences are brought to bear on us. Thus literature and the arts become of the greatest importance to us both as individuals and as members of society.

The poet is one who has a much wider field of stimulation than the ordinary man and one who is able to manage his impulses with less confusion. He is able to order experience because he is able to bring opposed impulses into equilibrium. Nothing can substitute for literature and the arts because the experiences they offer are rarely if ever obtainable elsewhere. Even the most adequately equipped persons cannot dispense with these experiences. Indeed, these people value them most.

Art's function is the widening and better ordering of human experiences. The more of the human personality that is engaged, the better the life. So it is that art and literature can lead to modes of mental organization that will enable us not only to live as better organized individuals but will lead to a society whose morality is more adaptable to the changing conditions of our time.

In judging actual works of literature, how are we to tell which are well organized and which are not? Mr. Richards suggests that we are refreshed if a work of literature is up to, or better than, our own level of organization and are depressed if it falls below it. But this is arguing in a circle, saying in effect that the well-organized person recognizes the well-organized work of art.

Yet Richards would probably be willing to rest his main argument on the contention that value is a quantitative matter and that, if the psychologist does not yet know how to make the measurements required, it is at least well to know what has to be measured.

BIBLIOGRAPHY

Ogden, C. K., and I. A. Richards. *The Meaning of Meaning: a Study of the Influence of Language Upon Thought and of the Science of Symbolism.* New York, 1936.
Pollock, T. C. *A Theory of Meaning Analyzed: a Critique of I. A. Richards' Theory of Language and Literature, Elementalism: the Effect of an Implicit Postulate of Identity on I. A. Richards' Theory of Poetic Value by J. G. Spaulding.* Chicago, 1942.
Richards, I. A. *The Philosophy of Rhetoric.* New York, 1936.
———. *Practical Criticism, a Study of Literary Judgment.* London, 1934.
———. *Principles of Literary Criticism.* 2nd ed. New York, 1926.

32 · T. S. Eliot (1888–   )

T. S. ELIOT has described himself as a classicist in literature, a royalist in politics, and an Anglo-Catholic in religion. Equalitarianism, progress, and liberalism are detested by him. He is, in more than the theological sense of the word, dogmatic, and he declares in one place that the only people who can understand what he is talking about are those for whom the doctrine of original sin is a very real and tremendous thing.

Throughout this survey of critical thought we have often noticed how intertwined a man's ideas about literature are with his social and religious thinking. Neoclassicism in the age of Louis XIV was part of the whole intellectual picture, a picture that included orthodoxy in religion and support of the monarch in politics. Whether the neoclassicists themselves are completely conscious of how their literary thinking complements their thinking in other realms may be doubted. Eliot, however, understands that his beliefs in politics, religion, and literature form a whole.

Though his ideas about individual literary figures have undergone metamorphoses throughout the years (his partial reversal on Milton is the most striking example), the general outline of his critical position has remained unchanged. The essays he wrote at the end of the First World War embody the same fundamental ideas as his later ones.

In 1917 he wrote an essay, "Tradition and the Individual Talent," which is still valuable as an introduction to his thought. It was written to combat the idea that a poet should be praised in proportion to his originality. No poet or artist of any sort can be understood solely in terms of himself. Often the most valuable parts of the poet's work are those in which "the dead poets, his ancestors, assert their immortality most vigorously." All the existing monuments of literature compose an order, an ideal form. Each new work alters, even if but slightly, the whole order. Thus it is that each new piece of work must inevitably be judged by the standards of the past. The poet must know the main current of literature. He must have "the historical sense, which we may call nearly indispensable to any one who would continue to be a poet beyond his twenty-fifth year." There is a mind outside of his own, the mind of Europe, of his own country. The conscious present is an awareness of the past. The dead writers are that which we know.

This mind of Europe (tradition is another word for it) is more important than the individual poet. He must subordinate himself to it because it is more valuable than his own personality. "The progress of the artist is a continual self-sacrifice, a continual extinction of personality."

To make clearer the relation of this process of depersonalization to the sense of tradition, Eliot gives as an analogy what happens when a piece of platinum is introduced into a gas chamber containing sulphur and carbon dioxide. The two gases then form sulphurous acid, but the platinum itself remains unchanged. The mind of the poet is the platinum. The emotions and feelings are the gases. The more perfect he is as a poet the less his own personality is involved. His mind forms the new compounds but he remains separate from what he creates. In great art, "the difference between art and the event is absolute."

What Eliot is directly attacking is the romantic notion that the poet expresses his personality. The experiences that are important for the poet as a man may have no place in his poetry, and those that are important in his poetry may have little or nothing to do with his personality.

Eliot writes that it is an error for the poet to feel that his own emotions are in any way remarkable or interesting. "The business of the poet is not to find new emotions, but to use ordinary ones, and, in working them up into poetry, to express feelings which are not in actual emotions at all. And emotions which he has never experienced will serve his turn as well as those familiar to him." Thus Wordsworth's "emotion recollected in tranquillity" cannot be accepted by Eliot. For the latter it is the concentration of a very great number of experiences, rather than emotions or recollections, that makes poetry. This concentration happens unconsciously. Naturally, though, a large part of the writing of poetry must be conscious. When the poet is unconscious when he ought to be conscious and conscious when he ought to be unconscious, he tends to be "personal," that is, a bad poet. "Poetry is not a turning loose of emotion but an escape from emotion; it is not expression of personality but an escape from personality. But, of course, only those who have personality and emotions know what it means to want to escape from these things."

It is to be feared that these last sentences are all too typical of Eliot as a critic. He makes large generalizations supported by few specific examples and wards off questions with a snobbish aside. You either agree with him, he says, or you demonstrate your inferiority. What he says in this essay has been said many times before by the neoclassicists, the "new humanists," and all those who are in opposition to individualism in poetry. The poet lives in a tradition; he must surrender himself to this tradition. "The emotion of art is impersonal."

In another essay, "The Function of Criticism," Eliot declares that the problem of criticism, like that of art, is essentially one of order. The true critic will subordinate his personal prejudices to the common pursuit of true judgment. He must have objective standards of value. In other words, he must support classicism, for "men cannot get on without giving allegiance to something outside of themselves." Romanticism is fragmentary, immature, and chaotic. Classicism is complete, adult, and orderly.

The "inner voice" must be rejected. This is mere nonconformism and Whiggism. The true critic must conform to orthodoxy because there are common principles, laws if you will, which it is his business to seek out. His must also have a highly developed sense of *fact*. Fact cannot corrupt taste. Opinion and fancy can. He must understand that "there is the possibility of co-operative activity, with the further possibility of arriving at something outside of ourselves, which may provisionally be called truth."

A later book, *Notes Towards the Definition of Culture* (1949), lets us know in bold terms that Eliot has no doubts. The title is not, one notices, notes toward "a" definition of culture, but towards "the" definition of culture. Throughout the book he speaks ex cathedra. He asserts that there are three conditions for culture. First, there must be a society in which culture is transmitted by heredity; this requires social classes. Second, the culture must contain within itself local cultures. Third, it must have within it a balance of unity and diversity in religion.

He argues that superior individuals, the elite, must be "formed into suitable groups, endowed with appropriate powers and perhaps with varied emoluments and honors." But this elite must be attached to some class or it will lack cohesiveness. What class this should be may be seen when he says that in a "healthily stratified society," the governing class will be those who inherit special advantages and who have a "stake in the country."

The strongest cultures are those which have dissent in the form of local or regional cultures. English culture would be weakened if there were not Scotch and Welsh cultures too.

As an example of unity and diversity in religion he points to the dominant cultural tradition as that of Rome, and the Church of England as the diverse element in a European sense. On the other hand, in Great Britain the Church of England is the dominant group, and diversity is brought about by the existence of the dissenting sects. In defending one's religion one defends one's culture. Methodism, for instance, played its part by keeping alive the culture of working-class Christians. Each stratum of society has its appropriate culture.

Without this triple stratification, the conditions for culture disappear. He who objects to Eliot's view of society is quickly put in his place. "If it seems monstrous to him that anyone should have 'advantages of birth', I do not ask him to change his faith, I merely ask him to stop paying lip-service to culture."

BIBLIOGRAPHY

Beer, Ernst. *Thomas Stearns Eliot und der Antiliberalismus des XX. Jahrhunderts.* Wien, 1953.

Brombert, V. H. *The Criticism of T. S. Eliot: Problems of an "Impersonal Theory" of Poetry.* New Haven, 1949.

Buckley, Vincent. *Poetry and Morality: Studies on the Criticism of Matthew Arnold, T. S. Eliot, and F. R. Leavis.* London, 1959.

Eliot, T. S. *Essays, Ancient and Modern.* London, 1936.

———. *The Frontiers of Criticism.* Minneapolis, 1956.

———. *Notes Towards the Definition of Culture.* London, 1948.

———. *On Poetry and Poets (Essays).* New York, 1957.

———. *Selected Essays.* New York, 1950.

Gallup, D. C. *T. S. Eliot: a Bibliography, Including Contributions to Periodicals and Foreign Translations.* 1st American ed., New York, 1953.

Lucy, Seán. *T. S. Eliot and the Idea of Tradition.* London, 1960.

Matthiessen, F. O. *The Achievement of T. S. Eliot: An Essay on the Nature of Poetry. With a Chapter on Eliot's Later Work by C. L. Barber.* 3rd ed. New York, 1958.

33 · The New Criticism

THE TREMENDOUS PRESTIGE of Eliot as a poet gave such weight to his critical opinions that the appearance of his collection of critical essays *The Sacred Wood* (1920) initiated a trend in modern aesthetics now known as the New Criticism. Though the term was used earlier by J. E. Spingarn, and though Paul Valéry had previously been polishing the same critical instruments in France, Eliot undoubtedly can be considered the father of this new school, particularly since the major practitioners have been either American or English.

As a descriptive term, "new criticism" is completely meaningless, since all criticism is "new" when it first appears. Further, if one takes it as applying to all modern critics one soon discovers that they differ so much among themselves that any simple definition of the school will exclude a number of important critics. One critic will emphasize close reading, another symbols, another morality, another psychology, another sociology, and still another the mythical.

Yet the historian of criticism cannot help suspect that a few generations from now the most disparate critics will be felt to resemble each other in much the same way as Rousseau and Voltaire, almost at opposite poles in their own lifetimes, are considered part and parcel of the same great age of French thought.

If one could hazard a guess as to what will one day seem common to this critical age it would be the assumption that literature is the most important of human activities. If theology was once considered the queen of the sciences, it was because man's relation to God was the overriding concern of the age of theology. If today a large number of thinkers look to literature to give life a meaning in an age when the older answers of religion and politics seem unsatisfactory, the present age might well be termed the age of criticism, as the earlier was called the age of theology. This analogy can be better understood if it is realized that, as in an age of theology in which the theologians may well differ on every point but the object of their concern, so may literary critics differ in an age of criticism.

Since literature itself has been their concern, many contemporary critics have shifted the spotlight from theories about literature to the individual texts themselves. The close analysis of the very texture of the poem or prose work has, of course, a long history which reaches from the Greeks and the Romans through the great teachers of the ancient classics and the French explicators of texts to the modern close readers. Unfortunately, though, there have been times when the study of literature has seemed to be the study of almost anything except the literary work itself, as we have seen in our chapters on Taine and Zola. Academic halls have seen lecturers whose major concern was history or biography or sociology or linguistics using literary texts as mere illustrations of their own subject. The most extreme reaction to this kind of thing was to deny that anything existed but the text itself. This led to a point of view which insisted on looking at the work of art as if it had been produced in a vacuum, as if, to give one example, the date when the work of art was produced was completely irrelevant to its understanding.

The lunatics on the fringe of this movement were sitting ducks for the fire of the traditionalists. These latter took malicious pleasure in exposing so-called "explications" which were based on, say, the explicator's ignorance of the fact that certain words in a seventeenth-century poem had meanings quite different from those they have today.

Up until a few years ago the battle between the New Critics and the traditionalists was fought with a bitterness that made any reconciliation seem impossible. Today, now that most of the dust has settled, one can see that the fire of both sides was concentrated on the extreme flanks of the enemy. The center of each army was left unscathed since, in truth, there was no fundamental disagreement between them.

This may be seen clearly in an essay by Cleanth Brooks, one of the pillars of the New Criticism. He begins an essay called "The Formalist Critic" (*The Kenyon Review*, 1951) as follows:

Here are some articles of faith I could subscribe to:

That literary criticism is a description and evaluation of its object.

That the primary concern of criticism is with the problem of unity . . . the kind of whole which the literary work forms or fails to form, and the relation of the various parts to each other in building up this whole.

That the formal relations in a work of literature may include, but certainly exceed, those of logic.

That in a successful work, form and content cannot be separated.

That form is meaning.

That literature is ultimately metaphorical and symbolic.

That the general and the universal are not seized upon by abstraction, but got at through the concrete and the particular.

That literature is not a surrogate for religion.

That as Allen Tate says, "specific moral problems" are the subject matter of literature, but that the purpose of literature is not to point a moral.

That the principles of criticism define the area relevant to literary criticism; they do not constitute a method for carrying out the criticism.

However, Brooks goes on from here to show his knowledge of the criticism of those who call themselves literary historians and literary biographers and gladly admits that man's "experience is a seamless garment, no part of which can be separated from the rest." If, in the end, he makes a modest apologia for the formalist approach, he generously admits that it is but one of many tools useful in understanding literature.

One example of the skillful use of this tool may be found in Allen Tate's essay "Tension in Poetry." (*Collected Essays*, 1959) Here is his reading of three lines from Dante's well-known Paolo and Francesca episode:

You will remember that when Dante first sees the lovers they are whirling in a high wind, the symbol of lust. When Francesca's conversation with the poet begins, the wind dies down and she tells him where she was born in these lines:

> *Siede la terra dove nata fui*
> *Sulla marina dove il Po discende*
> *Per aver pace co' seguaci sui.*

Courtney Landon renders the tercet:

> The town where I was born sits on the shore,
> Whither the Po descends to be at peace
> Together with the streams that follow him.

But it misses a good deal; it misses the force of "seguaci" by rendering it as a verb. Professor Grandgent translates the third line: "To have peace with its pursuers," and comments: "The tributaries are conceived as chasing the Po down to the sea." Precisely; for if the "seguaci" are merely followers, and not pursuers also, the wonderfully ordered density of this simple passage is sacrificed. For although Francesca has told Dante where she lives, in the most directly descriptive language possible, she has told him more than that. Without the least imposition of strain upon the firmly denoted natural setting, she fuses herself with the river Po near which she was born. By a subtle shift of focus we see the pursued river as Francesca in Hell: the pursuing tributaries are a new visual image for the pursuing winds of lust. A further glance yields even more: as the winds, so the tributaries at once pursue and become one with the pursued; that is to say, Francesca has completely absorbed the substance of her sin . . . she is the sin; as, I believe it is said, the damned of the Inferno are plenary incarnations of the sin that has put them there. The tributaries of the Po are not only the winds of lust by analogy of visual images; they become identified by means of sound:

> . . . *discende*
> *Per aver pace co' seguaci sui.*

The sibilants dominate the line; they are the hissing of the wind. But in the last line of the preceding tercet Francesca has been grateful that the wind has subsided so that she can be heard—

> *Mentre che il vento, come fa, si tace.*

After the wind has abated, then, we hear in the silence, for the first time, its hiss, in the susurration to the descending Po. The river is thus both a visual and an auditory image, and since Francesca is her sin and her sin is embodied in this image, we are entitled to say that it is a sin that we can both hear and see.

Enlightening as this reading is, it obviously, as Tate would be the first to admit, only begins to explain the lines. The learning of the medieval historian, the romance philologist, the theologian, and the Dante specialist must all be used if one wants to approach still closer to Dante's art.

The problem presented by these three simple lines is the problem facing the critic of literature at the present time. Engaging in more close analysis than did his predecessor of a generation ago, he will still have to make use of all learning in every branch of traditional scholarship before he will be satisfied that he has done his job properly.

Living with so long and varied a history of literary criticism behind him, the modern critic is unlikely to place himself finally in any one school. While rejecting the kind of vulgar relativism that would deny all standards, he is likely to make a synthesis of the best insights of all schools, and he will realize that those standards that help illuminate classical drama, say, are not necessarily the best for understanding a romantic lyric.

Finally, he will realize that, important as his activity is in helping the reader or spectator to approach closer to the individual literary masterpiece, he can never delude himself into thinking that his activity is the equivalent of the work of art itself. His job is to clear the underbrush away so that another may walk more easily through the forest.

BIBLIOGRAPHY

Blackmur, R. P. *Language as Gesture*. New York, 1953.

Burke, Kenneth. *The Philosophy of Literary Form: Studies in Symbolic Action*. New York, 1957.

Daiches, David. *Critical Approaches to Literature*. Englewood Cliffs, N. J., 1956.

Danziger, M. K., and W. S. Johnson. *An Introduction to Literary Criticism*. Boston, 1961.

Eliot, T. S. *The Frontiers of Criticism: A Lecture at the University of Minnesota*. Minneapolis, 1956.

Foster, R. J. *The New Romantics: a Reappraisal of the New Criticism*. Bloomington, Ind., 1962.

Frye, Northrop. *Anatomy of Criticism: Four Essays*. Princeton, 1957.

Goldberg, Gerald J., and N. M. Goldberg, eds. *The Modern Critical Spectrum*. Englewood Cliffs, N. J., 1962.

Hardison, O. B., Jr. *Modern Continental Literary Criticism.* New York, 1962.

Howe, Irving. *Modern Literary Criticism.* Boston, 1958.

Hyman, S. E. *The Armed Vision: a Study in the Methods of Modern Literary Criticism.* New York, 1948.

Krieger, Murray. *New Apologists for Poetry.* Minneapolis, 1956.

Milton, John. *Poems. With Essays in Analysis;* by Cleanth Brooks and J. E. Hardy. New York, 1951.

Ransom, J. C. *New Criticism.* Norfolk, Conn., 1941.

Rosenthal, M. L., and A. J. M. Smith. *Exploring Poetry.* New York, 1955.

Spitzer, Leo. *Linguistics and Literary History.* Princeton, 1948.

Stallman, R. W. *Critiques and Essays in Criticism.* New York, 1949.

Wheelwright, Philip. *Metaphor and Reality.* Bloomington, Ind., 1962.

Winters, Ivor. *The Function of Criticism: Problems and Exercises.* Denver, Colo., 1957.

Zabel, M. D., ed. *Literary Opinion in America; Essays Illustrating the Status, Methods, and Problems of Criticism in the United States in the Twentieth Century.* Revised Edition. New York, 1951.

Abrams, M. H. *The Mirror and the Lamp.* New York, 1953.

Alden, R. N., ed. *Critical Essays of the Early Nineteenth Century.* New York, 1921.

Allen, G. W., and H. H. Clark. *Literary Criticism: Pope to Croce.* New York, 1941; reprinted Detroit, 1962.

Atkins, J. W. H. *English Literary Criticism: the Medieval Phase.* Gloucester, Mass., 1961.

Auerbach, Erich. *Mimesis;* tr. by W. R. Trask. Princeton, 1953.

Bacci, Orazio. *La Critica letteraria. Storia dei generi letterari italiani.* Milan, 1910.

Bate, W. J., ed. *Criticism: The Major Texts.* New York, 1948; reprinted 1952.

Bosanquet, Bernard. *A History of Aesthetics.* New York, 1892.

Brown, C. A. *The Achievement of American Criticism: Representative Selections from Three Hundred Years of American Criticism.* New York, 1954.

Cargill, Oscar. *Intellectual America: Ideas on the March.* New York, 1959.

Carritt, E. F. *Philosophies of Beauty from Socrates to Robert Bridges.* Oxford, 1931.

Crane, R. S., and others. *Critics and Criticism, Ancient and Modern.* Chicago, 1952.

Eliot, T. S. *The Use of Poetry and the Use of Criticism: Studies in the Relation of Criticism to Poetry in England.* Cambridge, 1933.

Foerster, Norman. *American Criticism: A Study in Literary Theory from Poe to the Present.* New York, 1962.

178

Gilbert, A. H. *Literary Criticism: Plato to Dryden.* New York, 1940; reprinted Detroit, 1962.

Gilbert, K. E. and Helmut Kuhn. *A History of Esthetics.* Bloomington, Ind., 1953.

Glicksberg, C. I. *American Literary Criticism, 1900–1950.* New York, 1952.

Green, T. M. *The Arts and the Art of Criticism.* Princeton, 1947.

Levin, Harry, ed. *Perspectives of Criticism* [by] W. J. Bate and others, Cambridge, 1950.

Lieder, P. R., and Robert Withington. *The Art of Literary Criticism.* New York, 1941.

Munro, Thomas. *The Arts and Their Interrelations.* New York, 1949.

O'Connor, William V. *An Age of Criticism, 1900–1950.* Chicago, 1952.

Pritchard, J. P. *Criticism in America.* Norman, Okla., 1956.

Rader, Melvin, ed. *A Modern Book of Esthetics, An Anthology.* New York, 1952.

Saintsbury, George. *A History of Criticism and Literary Taste in Europe.* Vols. I, II, III. 4th ed. Edinburgh and London, 1949.

Schorer, Mark, J. Miles, and G. McKenzie, eds. *Criticism: The Foundations of Modern Literary Judgment.* New York, 1948.

Scott-James, R. A. *The Making of Literature.* London, 1936.

Shipley, J. T. *Quest for Literature: A Survey of Literary Criticism and the Theories of the Literary Forms.* New York, 1931.

———, ed. *Dictionary of World Literature: Criticism . . . Forms . . . Technique.* New York, 1943.

Smith, J. H., and E. W. Parks, eds. *The Great Critics: An Anthology of Literary Criticism.* New York, 1951.

Stallman, R. W. *Critiques and Essays in Criticism, 1920–1948, Representing the Achievement of Modern British and American Critics.* New York, 1949.

Warren, A. H., Jr. *English Poetic Theory, 1825–1865.* Princeton, 1950.

Weber, Eugen, ed. *Paths to the Present: Aspects of European*

Thought from Romanticism to Existentialism. New York, 1960.

Wellek, René. *A History of Modern Criticism, 1750–1950. I. The Later Eighteenth Century. II. The Romantic Age.* New Haven, 1955.

————, and Austin Warren. *Theory of Literature.* New York, 1956.

West, R. B., Jr. *Essays in Modern Literary Criticism.* New York, 1952.

Wimsatt, W. K., Jr., and Cleanth Brooks. *Literary Criticism: A Short History.* New York, 1957.

Zabel, M. D., ed. *Literary Opinion in America; Essays Illustrating the Status, Methods, and Problems of Criticism in the United States in the Twentieth Century.* Revised edition. New York, 1951.